Endorsements for
The Jews

"Reading this book will make your mother proud."

–Mark Cuban

"So good I'm thinking of converting!"

–Ken Jennings, Host of *Jeopardy!*,
Author of *Planet Funny*

"*The Jews* is not only incredibly readable and informative, but also laugh out loud funny. Kutner walks a tightrope of what could have either come off as dry history and/or offensive comedy, but instead, nails the landing. And yes, I did just mix my performative sports metaphors."

–Jonathan Kesselman, Writer/Director,
The Hebrew Hammer

"Hilarious, smart, and fearless, and there's even a musical number—this book totally checks all my Jew-boxes."

–Rachel Bloom, Creator/Star,
Crazy Ex-Girlfriend

"Wow! Kutner's extensive and comprehensive history of the Jews is a great gift for both Jews and non-Jews of all ages. The millennial saga of the Jews, presented through a humorous lens, is a great contribution to Jewish humor."

–Moshe Waldoks, Co-Editor,
The Big Book of Jewish Humor

"Funny, irreverent, and packed with both inventiveness and information, *The Jews* is a terrific way to get to know, well, Jews!"

–Rabbi David Wolpe

"I foresee great laughter in your future if you buy this book."

–Isaiah

THE JEWS

5,000 YEARS AND COUNTING

ROB KUTNER

WICKED SON

A WICKED SON BOOK
An Imprint of Post Hill Press
ISBN: 979-8-88845-350-6
ISBN (eBook): 979-8-88845-351-3

The Jews:
5,000 Years and Counting
© 2025 by Rob Kutner
All Rights Reserved

Cover Design by Jim Villaflores

Scripture quotations marked (JPS) are taken from the JPS Tanakh published 1917.

This book, as well as any other Wicked Son publications, may be purchased in bulk quantities at a special discounted rate. Contact orders@posthillpress.com for more information.

This is a work of nonfiction. All people, locations, events, and situations are portrayed to the best of the author's memory.

Post Hill Press
New York • Nashville
wickedsonbooks.com
posthillpress.com

Published in the United States of America
1 2 3 4 5 6 7 8 9 10

To all the Jews

Who, if history is any guide,

Could probably use a laugh right now

"*Properly, the Jew ought hardly to be heard of, but he is heard of, has always been heard of.... All things are mortal but the Jews; all other forces pass, but he remains.*"

—MARK TWAIN

"*Some people like the Jews, and some do not. But no thoughtful man can doubt the fact that they are beyond all question the most formidable and the most remarkable race which has ever appeared in the world.*"

—WINSTON CHURCHILL

"*They are a stiff-necked people.*"

—GOD

ILLUSTRATIONS

"Judge Samson" —Steven Gordon
"Arch of Titus" —David DeGrand
"Rabbi Action Cards" —Len Rodman
"The Jews Who Created The Movies:
The Movie" —Tim Wolkiewicz
"Memorial Wall" —Sasha Kutner
"Let's Eat" —Daria Hoffman with special thanks to
Sarah Benor and the Jewish Language Project

No Jews were harmed in the making of this book.
But that doesn't mean they won't complain.

TABLE OF CONTENTS

IN THE BEGINNING

SO THEN...THAT HAPPENED

IF NOT NOW, WHEN?

SO NOW WHAT?

INTRODUCTION

WHAT *IS* JEWISH HISTORY?

I know, I know, right now you're thinking, "Hey, what are you asking *me* for? Isn't this literally your job, Invisible Book Guy?" You might even be trying to get your money back forty words in. Wise move.

But if you've stuck around, it's a tricky question. Which is fine, because questions are the lifeblood of Judaism. Our Talmud is a collection of questions the size of a bookshelf, and approximately 90 percent of them never get resolved. Our Passover Seder is built around asking questions. Like scientists, we will never stop asking "How?" Like toddlers, we'll never stop asking "Why?" And like optometrists, "Better like this, or like this?"

However, unlike the Four Questions of the Seder (to which my grandpa Al of blessed memory would always append a fifth question: "When do we eat?"), the question of how to tell the story of the Jewish people defies easy answers.

Of course, the Hebrew Bible provides an incredibly detailed chronicle of the Jewish people spanning millennia, from Eve's first decision to get more produce into her diet to around 500 BCE, which is when the story of Purim took place (or at least what little participants could remember after that party). The only problem is that there's very little corroborating evidence. Which is frankly embarrassing for a people who've produced so many lawyers.

One complication is that, to use academic terminology, *it's all so friggin' old!* There is a smattering of archaeological clues, enough to establish that there have been Jews around the general Land-of-Israel vicinity for thousands of years. There are references to Jews in the fragmented histories of other communities we supposedly lived near, traded with, borrowed religious and cultural concepts from, intermarried with, and politely took turns conquering and being conquered by.

But at the end of the day, there's just no way to carbon-date Egypt getting smothered by frogs.

Then, when we move into an era with a bit more of an evidentiary record, there's the perennial challenge of "history is written by the victors." Which for most of our history, the Jews were—let's face it—*not*.

And finally, as we approach modern times, history itself—for everyone, not just the Jews—becomes more of a contested thing. Now the problem is the opposite of the first stage: there's *too much information*. Not like the kind your recently divorced dentist shares while you're trapped in a chair with sharp objects pointed at your gums. Too much of a *historical* record. There are so many accounts from, by, and about all kinds of people and happenings, that historians have to wrestle their way to something approaching "the truth." And if you've ever met a historian, most are not exactly in what you'd call "fighting shape."

Nevertheless, I'm going to make the effort.

Why? First of all, because if I don't, I'll be liable for breach of contract with my publisher.

But more to the point, because it's a hell of a tale. Murder! Treachery! Lust! Miracles! Kings! Wars! Rebellions! Courage!

Ingenuity! Resilience! Reinvention(s)! And *so* much…let's just call it "involuntary travel."

Jewish history is also compelling because it's drastically unlike any other history. No other people repeatedly exiled from their land has held onto a single national identity as long, has survived so many attempts to deliberately eliminate it—and still continues to fight over who actually belongs to it.

Our history also carries the very healthy reminder to not get too attached to any particular institution, empire, or way of life. Nothing is permanent, all is an illusion…wait a minute, now I'm veering into Buddhism.

Finally, I think it's critical for Jews to know our history because it still very much defines who we are today. Almost every issue that affects Jews nowadays is colored, consciously or subconsciously, by our long and specific history of travails, triumphs, and stubborn independence. We are marked by battle scar upon battle scar. Just don't show them to our mothers—you know they worry.

Will I get it right? I'm sure the historians will say no. Again, though, I can probably take them in a fight.

But here's the good news: I've gotten help.

Not the therapeutic kind I'm often being urged (and occasionally court-ordered) to seek, but help telling the story. For you see, I recently happened upon a treasure trove of previously "lost" documents that reveal certain chapters of Jewish history from *those who were actually there*. So in between my attempts to tell the story, I'll frequently step aside and let them do the talking. That's right. Even Jewish documents love to talk.

Incidentally, that means that if you think this book is too religious, or is too *sac*rilegious, or leans too far right, or leans too far left, or leaves out your specific Jewish subgroup, or talks about too many Jewish sub-sub-sub-groups, or somehow achieves all of the above at once...don't blame me. Blame the meddling Mesopotamian housewives, undying psychoanalysts, texting Spanish Inquisitioners, singing immigrants, and various other personalities and document-hoarders who supplied me with these completely real and in no way made-up accounts.

So let's dive into it. Starting at the only sensible place to begin a story...

IN THE BEGINNING

CREATION

A SNAKE'S-EYE VIEW

HEY THERE. SSSALUTATIONS! SORRY, SNAKE humor. That's right, I'm The Snake, from the original biblical tale in the book of Genesis. You know, the wily, smooth-talking reptile who tempted Adam and Eve into violating God's very first instruction?

And for my notorious role in history, I have two words I'd like to say to all of humanity, past, present and future:

You're welcome.

Because without me, none of the good stuff would have happened.

We all know the basic storyline. First there was nothing (or technically, "void and waste"), then God got to work and started creatin': light, sky, land, seas, plants, birds, fish, insects, cosmological bodies, and furry bodies. Then God created the first man, Adam, and—immediately realizing that the guy was just a *bucket* of neediness—created Eve, a female companion for him. It was history's first blind date, complete with God overenthusiastically telling them, "You two have *so much in common*…"

Then God informed the pair that they could eat anything in the Garden of Eden *except* the fruit from one tree, the Tree of Knowledge of Good and Evil. Humans wouldn't even be Jews for thousands of years but were already getting stuck with their first rule on what not to eat.

More broadly, though, it was humanity's very first test of obedience to God, a critical pattern-setter for the relationship between people and God for all times.

Spoiler Alert: The pattern? Not good.

But here's the thing: How do you *truly* test someone's obedience unless the temptation is strong? Now look, maybe fruit from a tree that grows "The Knowledge of Good and Evil" sounds mouth-watering to *you*, but even non-figuratively, it was basically just an apple. According to some rabbis, maybe it was even a fig, date, or stalk of wheat—even less delicious raw foods. Worth defying the Creator for? Probably not.

So that's where I came in.

I talked up that fruit to Eve, told her how delicious it was, suggested that the downside of disobeying God wasn't *that bad*. Admittedly, it's not that hard to deceive a naïve being who's one day old, but I pulled out all the stops. I improvised a tragic backstory about how not eating this fruit killed my father. I lowered my voice and did a scary gravelly voice when pretending to be God. I even got her to do a little light role-playing ("OK, this time, I'll play the mouth…")

Why did I do it? If I'm being honest, living in a place of complete, wall-to-wall perfection is *boring as sin*. I could feel that even before there was such a thing as sin.

But more to the point, from where I slither, the Jewish people have always placed a premium on the acquisition of knowledge. Which is something to be proud of. Did you really want to go through history known primarily as "The Naked People Who Don't Eat Apples?"

So essentially, I told Eve, "Go on. Have a Cheat Day."

And it worked! Eve took a bite, shared the fruit with Adam, and the deed was done. Humankind had made a first bold, adolescent step of independence from its parent. It was pretty much the only way they could act out in a time before there were cigarettes and there was really no way to sleep around.

It gets better. Now armed with The Knowledge of Good and Evil—and the freewill to choose between them—humanity entered a much deeper relationship with God. Now instead of humans just being stuck in their leafy prison, they would be free to roam about the whole planet—and it would be up to God to provide people with moral and behavioral guidelines. For the Jews, this took the form of the Ten Commandments, the Torah, the Mishna, the Gemara, and the millennia of scholarship that followed. A.k.a., the key branding elements of "The Jewish Experience."

But what about all the bad stuff that came next? God banished Adam and Eve from the Garden, forced men to labor in the soil to grow their food, and made it so women would experience labor pains when giving birth. Now come on, that's not on you. That's just God being bitter about human independence and the people who help bring forth life. So I don't call it banishment, I call it the "Snake's Guaranteed Employment For Farmhands and Obstetricians Act."

So in sum: Because of me, there would one day arise a people famous for challenging authority, seeking knowledge, delving deeply into ethical dilemmas, and—often as a result of knowing too much—repeatedly getting kicked out of where they're living.

Not bad for a creature who can't even use chopsticks!

THE FLOOD

ACCORDING TO NOAH'S WIFE

I SUPPOSE IT'S PARTIALLY MY fault since I insisted that he get a hobby.

But after 480 years being married to the same guy, can you blame me?

The name's Naamah, by the way. You may know my more famous husband, Noah. A guy whom the Torah describes as "blameless in his generation" and I describe as capital B BORING! All day long, century in, century out, he's puttering around the house, working on various "home improvements." We lived in a one-room clay shack in a time before windows, central AC, or indoor plumbing. How much was there to improve?

So when Noah came in one day saying, "The Creator of the Universe just spoke to me," of course I perked up. Finally, after endless gossip about neighbors we kept outliving, inside jokes that lasted longer than many dynasties, and repeatedly traded questions of "How's *your* lentil stew?" we had something to talk about!

"The *Creator of the Universe*!" I gasped. "What did he have to say???"

"Looks like rain."

Basically, the Lord was experiencing something called "Creator's Regret." Specifically, about us humans. We were bad. We were violent. Each person was a law onto themselves.

Or as God looked at it, we were apparently just too *dry*.

So God tells the hubs, "I'm going to wash this species right off of my globe. And you're gonna have to build a giant rescue boat called an ark." And miraculously, Noah did so without accidentally leaving any spare "ark parts" out. So now I'm trying to talk myself into this: "It won't be so bad—I've always wanted to go on a cruise…"

Then came the part about the animals.

Apparently, we would be joined on this little jaunt by two of every animal species so they could repopulate the entire planet afterwards. No pressure, guys!

So the animals came, then the rains, and before we knew it, we were all locked in there together. I mean, granted, every mother wants to spend more time with her kids, and I'm sure my giraffe and llama counterparts agreed. But still, it was forty days of rain, then almost another year of just…floating. During all of which, I'm proud to report, I didn't get seasick once.

Just nauseous every morning from the stench of all those animals eating, excreting, and um…possibly doing things to speed up the repopulation of the Earth.

Soon enough, though, the rains had abated, the land had dried, and our little Wooden Box of Stank came to rest on top of a mountain. Which, between you and me, is really *not* the most convenient place to park a boat.

But no complaints here! I was just glad it was all finally over, which God let us definitively know by creating the rainbow. (Personally, I found the color scheme a little "busy," but who am I to quibble with the Designer of the Universe?) Then it was time to let the animals out to refill the Earth and for us to rebuild human society, humans who would one day give rise to the Jewish people.

But first, we were going to need a *lot* of towels.

THE PATRIARCHS & MATRIARCHS
...IN THERAPY

DR. COHEN: Alright, everyone, why don't we get started? I know that some of you did not live at the same time as each other, but as a famous rabbinic commentator once said, "There is no chronology in the Torah." Isaac, I believe you had something you wanted to address?

ISAAC: I do, Doc. Just a little thing that keeps bugging me called (to Abraham): *You tried to kill me, dude!*

SARAH: Seriously, Abe! It took me almost a century to get pregnant with him!

ABRAHAM: Whoa whoa whoa, I'm feeling a little *attacked* here.

ISAAC: You mean like me, *tied up on that rock?*

ABRAHAM: Hey, try and see it from my perspective. I'm the founder of Judaism. This guy God contacts me, saying, "We're starting up something new, and I want you in on the ground floor. But first, there's some stuff you've gotta do." How am I supposed to refuse a direct order from my all-powerful boss?

DR. COHEN: So, what I'm hearing here is a problem with boundaries?

JACOB: Guys, give Grandpa a break! You know, there's a lot of pressure on us "Leading a whole clan around the desert" guys…

ISAAC: Oh, now *you're* going to claim the moral high ground, Mr. Swindle-My-Brother-and-Trick-My-Blind-Dad-Into-Giving-Me-His-Blessing-On-His-Deathbed?

JACOB: Hey! I spent the rest of *my* life getting deceived and manipulated as payback for that. You know how my uncle cheated me, and what my other sons did to my favorite, Joseph, selling him into slavery and making me think he was dead. Besides…it was Mom's idea!

REBECCA: Baby, you *had* to get that blessing to carry on the Jewish line. Mother knows best.

ISAAC: Yes, because what better way to establish ourselves as a people of law, ethics, and higher values than stealing something promised to your brother and deceiving your blind father?

DR. COHEN (nodding sympathetically): It's hard being the "Middle Patriarch."

ISHMAEL: Oh, you're one to complain. Mom and I got cast out and had to wander around the desert on camels for the rest of our lives. No one even sent us a postcard.

ESAU: Nobody ever asks my opinion either. That soup was cold, and it could have used more salt. Can I get a do-over?

JACOB: Hey, a deal's a deal. Use a better lawyer next time.

LEAH: Uh, can *I* get a word in edgewise? Try being immortalized throughout history as "the ugly one" and my husband's *second choice*!

RACHEL: Hold on a minute, sis. I know Jacob likes me better. But for a Biblical wife, that ain't worth squat if you're not producing heirs. How do you think it felt for me, watching you pop out babies like sunflower seeds while I only had two?

JOSEPH: Mom! Aunt Leah! Please! Can't we stop fighting, and focus on what really matters?

DR. COHEN: What's that, Joseph?

JOSEPH: The fact that, in the end, I was right. My prophetic dreams came true, and my brothers had to bow down to me as Chief Steward of Egypt.

RUBEN: Really, bro? Is that your title?

SHIMON: We forgot because you haven't mentioned it in at least ten seconds!

LEVI: I wouldn't boast if I were you. Because of you, our descendants ended up as slaves building the pyramids.

DR. COHEN: OK! I'm feeling a lot of negativity here. Why don't we go around and each say something we're grateful for? Who wants to go first?

ABRAHAM: I will! I'm grateful for a God who…likes being argued with.

ISAAC: Oh, so you were *fine* arguing with God not to kill some innocent strangers in Sodom and Gomorrah, but when it comes to *your own kid*...?

DR. COHEN: Isaac, Isaac. We need to let go of our traumas in order to heal.

ISAAC: (Sighs.) Fine. I'm grateful for...that ram you killed instead of me.

JACOB: I'm grateful to have thirteen beautiful children, two wives, two concubines...and many tents and flocks. It's good to be the patriarch!

REBECCA: I'm grateful to have actually had an impact on my son's career.

LEAH: I'm grateful for the ability to pop out babies as easy as spitting out sunflower seeds. Oops! Think I just had another right now!

RACHEL: What?!?

LEAH: Ha! Gotcha!

RACHEL: I'm grateful for...a husband willing to put in fourteen years of hard labor for me. It's so romantic. Where are all the real men these days?

RUBEN, SHIMON, LEVI, JUDAH, DAN, NAFTALI, GAD, ASHER, ISSACHAR, ZEVULUN, BENJAMIN, and DINA: Hey, we've barely gotten to speak. Can we just say—?

DR. COHEN: Sorry, out of time!

Dr. Cohen hustles them out the door and lets in two new patients, one of them severely bloodied.

DR. COHEN: Cain, Abel, come on in. I believe we were going to talk about "closure?"

THE SECRET DIARIES

....

Dear Diary,

Sometimes it's weird being the Prince of Egypt. Especially when the king isn't even your real dad.

I mean sure, there *is* the boundless wealth and luxury, unlimited use of "Dad"'s chariot, and free access to the pyramids 24/7.

Still, even that gets weird. Take the pyramids. I go out to see one, and there's all those Hebrew slaves blocking my view. And when I get in closer, I notice their stench too. Hello? We live *right next to the Nile.* Ever hear of soap?

But then one day I'm scrolling through the latest social media–glyphics and start seeing images and stories about what their lives are like. And I start thinking, "Those Hebrews are making me feel bummed about *my* life."

Then I dig deeper and learn about their struggle against oppression. And I decide that they need someone to fight their oppressors. And, with my copious amount of free time (#PrinceLife), that someone has got to be me.

I suppose I could have researched a bit more about these "Hebrews" or their complex 400-year history in Egypt, but hey, it's more fun to just get up and yell things.

So I go to "Dad," and I recite a slogan I saw on the 'glyphs in a really snazzy font being mouthed by a camel: "Decolonize your pyramids!"

But all he says is, "No!" Which, if you've ever spoken to Pharaoh, is kind of like his catchphrase.

So I try the line I usually use on him: "You're not even my *real* dad." Which doesn't work either. But it does get me wondering...

~

Dear Diary,

Well, today did not quite end up the way as I had planned! Or where.

I woke up this morning, so fired up with my newfound calling as The Savior™, I could hardly stay in bed past eleven!

Soon I was out amongst the Hebrews, dressing just like them (a few drops from the Nile helped complete the "sweaty from toil" effect), carrying signs that were covered with angry words, and even drawings of me making my best angry face.

But for some reason, the slaves wouldn't join me in my almost totally rhyming chants. Come on, guys—I had my royal servants workshop those for at least an hour! They also wouldn't join me in my protest marches—kept saying something about "these pyramids aren't going to build themselves"? People always have all kinds of excuses not to take up activism.

And then, all of a sudden, it got real.

I saw one of the Egyptian taskmasters beating up a Hebrew in a way that made me feel like this was very much not a safe space. So, as is my lifelong penchant (at least since yesterday), I took action!

I grabbed one of the bricks from my fellow Oppressed Folks, eliciting an annoyed "Hey!" and bonked that representative of The Man on the head. Apparently, I did a really good job and deserve a trophy because he just lay there on the ground and didn't get up or beat anyone else.

But not only did they *not* give me a trophy, my so-called former "allies" sent me packing! They said I had killed the guy (such aggressive language!) and that I had better clear out of Egypt before the same was done to me by Dad's law enforcement officials.

Well, everyone knows how I feel about cops! So out of Egypt I fled.

~

Dear Diary,

Whew! Life changes piling up for old Moses here. After fleeing from Egypt to convenient nearby Midian, I ended up at a well. And as I've learned from the ancient Hebrew tales, that's the best place to find the ladies.

And those tales were correct! I met a lovely young woman named Tzipporah, we got married, and I settled into my new career at her father's company as "VP of Shepherding." Little nepotism? What can I say, it's how I grew up.

Then, one day I'm out at work, keepin' it woolly, when I hear a voice!

And that is something you do *not* want to hear in my field. Shepherding is a solitary enterprise. If you start hearing another voice besides yours, and it's saying anything but "Baaa," that might be a sign you're losing it. Now the good news on the Moses's-mental-health front is that this voice was *definitely* not from a sheep.

The bad news? It was coming from a bush.

And it was calling my name.

Oh yes, and did I mention the bush also appeared to be on fire, yet not burning up? So...that really wasn't helping either! It made me miss one of the perks of Egyptian princedom: amazing health care coverage.

Nonetheless, eventually my curiosity overcame my anxieties about my noggin. I approached the bush, so I could hear what it was saying. I have to admit, I was not prepared for the thundering, history-altering words that came out of it next:

"Take off your shoes."

Alright, alright, I might be losing it, but when you live in a desert clime, you *never* mind an invitation to take off your shoes. I kicked off my sandals, relaxed a little, and freed my mind for whatever the bush had to say next.

"I am the God of your ancestors Abraham, Isaac, and Jacob!"

O-K, Mr. Name Dropper!

But before I could wonder whether maybe I had inhaled too much of the smoke coming out of that Godbush, it had a mission for me.

I was to go back to Egypt and liberate the Hebrew slaves because I was from the same people as them. It was literally my destiny to be this oppressed people's savior! Only now I had to do it God's way—by going directly to Pharaoh (not my now-dead not-my-dad but a new one I didn't even know. Don't ask. It's complicated.) And to make me more persuasive, God said I could pull out my shepherd's rod before Pharaoh, and it would perform miracles!

Even so, it all sounded totally terrifying, especially since I have a fear of public speaking. But Godbush told me that my apparently long-lost brother Aaron would help. And advised me to "just try picturing Pharaoh and all his courtiers naked."

Um, thanks but no thanks, God. I'd rather be the only one pulling out a rod.

THE JEWS

~

Dear Diary,

Well, that went better than expected!

Maybe this whole "being a leader" thing is starting to make me level up as a man. Or maybe it's the fact that, in addition to the magic rod and my brother with the gift of gab, God also had some pretty snazzy special effects lined up. Special effects persuasive enough to impress Pharaoh into immediately "downsizing" his free labor force.

Basically, the plan was that Pharaoh would refuse this request ten times, and then God would unleash ten escalating divine "plagues" that would forever enshrine God in legend as the Ruler of all Creation. Not to mention a genius at branding!

Here they were, in order of appearance:

- Turning all of Egypt's water to blood (good luck hydrating now!)

- An army of frogs (just to amuse future generations)

- A lice outbreak (and not just on the first day of school)

- Flies, like *everywhere* (yes, even in *those* places, pervs)

- Cattle disease (deadly, not like "cattle eczema")

- Skin boils (also not great for the first day of school)

- Hail (already unlikely enough in desert-locked Egypt, but these hailstones also had balls of fire inside them!)

- Enough locusts to eat up all their crops (except, of course, locusts who were avoiding carbs)

- Constant darkness (to the point where even candle sellers were like, "Enough! We're *too* rich!")

- The killing of their firstborn children (not engineered by "middle children," I swear)

Honestly? God could have probably sealed the deal by starting with number ten. But everyone loves a good story, and this one ended very well for us. See ya later, Egypt!

~

Dear Diary,

Sorry that I haven't been able to write much.. I'm kind of in "perma-travel" mode now. After the last plague, the Egyptians sent us packing, and the Hebrews marched away as free people, unburdened by slavery, headed straight to the land promised to our ancestors.

Except, there was this highly inconvenient body of water right in our way. And behind us, Pharaoh had reneged on his deal and come chasing after us with his army, pleading, "Come back, baby—I swear I'll change!"

Well fortunately, God still had a few shekels left in the special effects budget, and He told me to wave my staff over the Red Sea. And a dry path opened up before us! With the rest of the sea somehow held up in place on both sides, forming massive watery walls for us to walk in between. A miraculous way to escape Pharaoh's army and also get in some "horizontal fishing."

With the exception of a few Israelites (as we now called ourselves) who attempted to surf those "sick waves," we all made it safely across. And when Pharaoh's army attempted to follow, God caused their embarrassingly non-all-terrain chariot wheels to get stuck and the water-walls to collapse onto them. We were finally, decisively free from Egypt!

And then my sister Miriam and I pulled out some songs of celebration. You should have seen this wet, sandy batch of ex-slaves party like there was no tomorrow.

I mean, it's not like we had to get up for work in the morning...

~

Dear Diary,

Ingrates.

Despite all the amazing things God has done for them, these people keep finding "constant wandering in a desert" to be not the lifestyle they wanted. Even when God literally pulls out even more miracles in response to their complaints. They needed directions? God created a pillar of fire and cloud to lead them. They were thirsty? God enabled me to turn a rock into a water fountain. They got hungry? God provided them plenteous food called *manna*, literally from the sky. To which their response was, "Where's the meat?"

On the plus side, the Jews are finally starting to develop a cohesive national identity: the people who kvetch about food.

~

Dear Diary,

Just when I thought getting out of Egypt was as dramatic as it gets, we hit Mount Sinai.

Now, of course, this was God's plan all along. Before we could inhabit our new land and fully become a people, we needed an instruction manual. So we camped out, I did some rock-climbing, and soon God had gifted me with two stone tablets. Basically, a starter set of "Thou Shalt Dos and Don'ts" for becoming an ethical community, a strong nation, and a people loyal to their God.

About that last thing...

You see, I was up on that mountaintop a long time. Forty days, to be precise. For a people stuck in a desert with literally nothing to do, that was apparently too long. They started to wonder if I'd ever come back or if I had skipped town and was off summoning divine frog-swarms on another country.

And, despite witnessing miracles that would be talked about for millennia to come, they'd begun to doubt this immaterial God. All it took was four cups of wine, and suddenly they were like, "I'm just not seeing it." Which is *kinda the point?*

So I came down the mountain—no easy task when you're powerlifting two giant instruction stones—only to find that the people had gone ahead and made themselves an idol to worship: a calf made of gold. Because nothing strikes fear and awe into the faithful like an *adorable shiny baby animal.*

Let's just say I may have experienced some "anger management" issues.

Next thing I knew, God's words were on the mountainside, reduced to law-dust staining my toes. And I may have ordered the slaughter of a few Israelites. OK, maybe more than a few. Like I said, it's something I'm working through.

Fortunately, God gave them a second chance, and just a scant forty days later, I presented the people with the Ten Commandments 2.0. And this time...it was just easy. The people accepted it and said, "Everything that the Lord has commanded, we shall do."

Would it have killed them to say that *before* my toes got all law-dust-stained?

~

Dear Diary,

We made it! To the border of the Promised Land! So now we get to fulfill our destiny and march right in. We're so close I can practically taste the milk and honey...when a couple of Jews start talking. Which is never a good thing.

They ask, "How do we *know* we'll be able to conquer this land?" They want to do more research, or as I call it, "Jew diligence" (Hey, there's nothing in the Ten Commandments forbidding dad jokes.)

So, God and I reluctantly agree to let them send twelve men, one from each tribe, to scout the land out. And all but two of them come back, surprise surprise, kvetching. "The inhabitants are too big, too strong! We felt like grasshoppers compared to them!"

Hey, did you guys remember the God who literally controls entire swarms of locusts, flies, and lice? That's the one on *your* side, Grasshopper.

But it was too late. God was mad at their lack of faith, and essentially called their bluff, saying, "You're afraid you're going to die out, rather than take the Land? So be it. You all get to wander around the desert for forty years until this generation dies out."

Wow, and I thought *I* had anger issues.

MOSES

~

Dear Diary,

About that last thing...

Well, I guess this time I heard one kvetch more than I could take. The people were grousing about being thirsty again, which is the main thing they usually say besides "Are we there yet?"

God tells me, "Use your trusty staff to call forth water from that rock." So I do that, but I'm so peeved, I insult the people, take credit for the water-bringing myself, and instead of just using words, I strike the rock. Really badly.

So, God decides to deny me my all-access pass to the Land. And I'm told the time and place of my death: Mount Nebo, which at least has a nice view of the Land. Perfectly positioned for me to watch them enter, under the leadership of my appointed replacement Joshua, and yell—in proper Jewish fashion—"You're doing it wrong!"

Until then, I'm officially signing off here, Diary, to retire and write my memoirs. I've got a book in me that I'm pretty sure could one day be part of a global bestseller!

Warmly (and non-complainingly),
Moses

JUDGED

FROM 1150–1025 BCE, THE JEWISH *people inhabited the land of Israel but did not have a centralized government. Rather, they existed as a loose confederation of tribes, governed by a series of leaders known as "judges." There were twelve in all, and their stories fill the book of the Bible creatively titled "Judges."*

But why should the judges have all the fun? We now take a closer take a look at two of the most famous ones...in extremely judgmental fashion.

DEBORAH

Deborah was the fourth Judge of Israel, and the only female one. And for most of her judgeship, she preferred to sit under a date palm tree, forcing any disputant with a legal claim or conflict to come to her.

Girl, get your butt off the ground before you get splattered with bird poop! You think this young nation—which can't seem to do anything but complain and argue—is going to judge itself?

One day, Deborah learned that the Israelites' longstanding enemy, the Canaanites, threatened to invade. So she told the Israelite general Barak to prepare 10,000 men to fight. Barak pleaded for Deborah to come lead them, but she responded, "If I do, all the glory for this victory will go to a woman."

Ouch! Gender shame much, Deb? Also, seriously, how good is this date palm tree that you won't even leave it for a war? The only nemesis that a bunch of dates are equipped to fight is "post-Passover constipation."

Nonetheless, Deborah finally gave in to Barak and oversaw the defeat of the Canaanites and their general, Sisera. And as a result of this military victory, there was peace in the land for forty years.

Bo-ring!

SAMSON

During a time when Israel was at constant war with the Philistines, a man named Manoah and his wife Zorah were unable to have a baby. Then an Angel of the Lord came to tell them they would soon have a son who would deliver Israel from their foe. But there was one condition: Mom would have to dedicate the boy to public service and raise him as a "Nazirite," those who honor God by abstaining from wine and never shaving or cutting their hair.

Can't look at his face in a mirror, can't hold his liquor, and can't get a job without his Mommy's help. Is there anything this guy can do?

The boy, Samson, grew to manhood, and he possessed superhuman strength...and subhuman impulse control. He fell in love with a Philistine girl and set out to marry her despite his family's objections. But on the way to the wedding, a lion crossed his path. Samson literally ripped the lion in half and continued on his way.

You monster! That lion had a family...we're guessing. Not really a lot of "single lions" out there on the dating scene.

Then, at his wedding feast, Samson challenged his thirty Philistine groomsmen to answer a riddle, offering them thirty garments if they could solve it. When they did so by cheating, he killed thirty other Philistines and gave their garments to the groomsmen.

Oh please, Sam, regifting clothes as a wedding favor? That is so uncouth, even for a group of literal Philistines.

However, his father-in-law reneged on the bride betrothed to Samson, offering him a younger sister to marry instead. Samson did not like this and retaliated by tying torches to the tails of three hundred foxes, then sending them out to burn down a grain field. Later, Samson got into even more trouble with the Philistines, eventually killing 1,000 of them using only the jawbone of a donkey.

Just wondering: Did this guy ever actually do any, you know, judging?

Samson then fell for another woman named Delilah. And by then, he was a very wanted man by the Philistines. But there was just one problem: He was unstoppable. So, they persuaded Delilah to tie him up and reveal the secret to his strength. Samson fell for her tricks a solid three times! Finally, he gave in and admitted to Delilah that he would lose his strength if his hair was cut. Which the Philistines immediately did.

So let me get this straight: God miraculously gives a barren woman a baby for the express purpose of keeping the Israelites safe from a menacing foe. And he gives up his military advantage to that foe because he gets tricked by a girl? And this guy goes down in history for his...judgment?

The newly weakened Samson was imprisoned by the Philistines, who planned to humiliate him in a public spectacle at their temple. However, by the time this happened, Samson had grown his hair back. He used his regained strength to bring the temple roof crashing down, killing everyone inside…including himself.

Wow, someone *couldn't figure out how to deal with stage fright.*

According to the Bible, Samson was the last of the Judges.

Good riddance. Don't let the door hit your unshaven butt on the way out!

Coming to a TV screen near you...never.

GOD'S KNOW-IT-ALLS

NOWADAYS, THE WORD "PROPHET" IS used pretty loosely, to describe someone who's managed to have two lucky years on Wall Street or the astonishing supernatural foresight to predict "low-rise jeans are coming back!" But in biblical times, it specifically meant someone who had been in contact with the divine, whether through direct speech, dreams, metaphorical visions, or just general "God vibes."

And in Jewish tradition, prophets generally fall into four categories (although some of them pull double duty):

THE PART-TIMERS

These are the folks who attained a measure of divine insight but are better known for doing something else.

TYPICAL SAYING: "Oh man, I'm so wiped from work, I *totally* forget to prophesy today!"

MOST FAMOUS MEMBERS: Abraham, Sarah, Isaac, Jacob, Moses, Aaron, Miriam, Joshua, King David, King Solomon, and Queen Esther.

Oddly, Joseph is only regarded as a prophet by Islam and Christianity, despite fulfilling the two cardinal rules of Jewish prophecy:

1) *What you prophesied came true* (which happened over and over to Joseph, from his ascension over his family

to the seven-year famine that he averted for Egypt. Less successful were his warnings to future Jewish workers to avoid "pyramid schemes").

2) *What you prophesy does not violate the laws of the Torah* (which he did not, unless there's a song I'm forgetting from *Joseph and The Amazing Technicolor Dreamcoat* extolling the praises of bacon).

THE GADFLIES

The role of a king in ancient Israel was...problematic. It's something God never wanted; the people demanded it "in order to be like the other nations" (hey, Israel was still adolescent and vulnerable to peer pressure). And many kings and queens had a habit of getting corrupt and falling for Literally Any Religion Besides Judaism.

Enter the Gadfly Prophet, sent by God to remind the king (and nation) of their roots, of their covenant with God, and of their values. They were like God's "tough love" coaches, a one-person intervention for monarchs addicted to their own power—only without the chariot outside waiting to take you to rehab.

TYPICAL SAYING: "Your Majesty, please do not force the God of Abraham, Isaac, and Jacob and omnipotent Creator of the Universe to 'take His belt off.'"

MOST FAMOUS MEMBERS: Samuel (Gadfly to King Saul), Nathan (to King David), Elijah (to King Ahab and Queen Jezebel), Jeremiah (to Kings Jehoiakim and Zedekiah), and Amos (to Kings Uzziah and Jeroboam).

THE QUOTABLES

These are the heavy hitters, the ones whose soaring poetry have the power to make us feel incredibly inspired or awful even today. They are the tequila of theology.

Although many also operated as Gadflies within their political regimes, their message to the people of Israel—then and now—often transcends the day-to-day. They slammed the rich and powerful for being hypocritically pious with religious ritual while oppressing the poor. Or as today's elite would call it, "multitasking."

They conjured up graphically detailed, terrifying punishments that God would unleash upon Israel and other nations. Some of those are still cited today by clergy seeking to instill their congregations with fear or relieve them of cash.

They also invoke magisterial visions of world peace, when "the wolf shall dwell with the lamb, the leopard lie down with the kid" (Isaiah 11:6, JPS) and other rooming arrangements that would definitely not be up to code. Some of these visions have been co-opted by Christians as referring to the anticipated birth of Jesus. Others have offered the hope of salvation and a messianic future redemption to the Jews during particularly dark times—that is, approximately every twenty years.

TYPICAL SAYING: "I hope you're sitting down for this next part..."

FAMOUS MEMBERS: Isaiah, Micah, Jeremiah, Amos—pretty much any name of a boy who's been homeschooled.

THE DRAMA QUEENS

These were the ones whose prophesying included some rather "cinematic" turns.

Jonah

Like many prophets, Jonah was just a regular guy whom God called upon to get the word out. However, his storyline was atypical in three ways:

1) *He was sent to prophesy to non-Jews*—specifically, the people of Nineveh, in what is now Iraq. He was supposed to tell them they had forty days to repent from their wicked ways or God would destroy their city. Other prophets reference and address other nations, but Jonah is the only one whose entire calling was 100 percent "*goyim*-focused."

2) *He refused the call*—infamously fleeing in the opposite direction from Nineveh and attempting to escape God's reach by taking a ship out to sea, where he thought God wouldn't follow him. Apparently, he mistook God for a swarm of bees.

3) *He got swallowed!* Not actually by a whale—the text calls it simply a "big fish." It is for this reason that Jews to this day take revenge on fish by chopping it into grey mushy ellipsoids that accumulate a weird jelly and sometimes a slice of carrot.

Elijah

I didn't want to have to break this to you here, but, according to the Hebrew Bible (or Tanakh), in the tenth century BCE, the nation of Israel had a divorce. And no, it wasn't your fault.

We'll soon learn more about the reasons why, but basically Israel split into a Northern and Southern Kingdom. It's a bit like if the US Civil War had taken place 3,000 years ago (or, approximately how long it will take the US South to get over it).

This division meant that the Northern Kingdom got their own set of kings and queens. And under King Ahab and Queen Jezebel, they utterly abandoned the traditional worship of one, invisible, monotheistic God at the Temple. This was, in part, because that Temple was inconveniently located in the Southern Kingdom. Clearly the North should have hired a better divorce lawyer and fought for at least weekend visitation.

Ahab and Jezebel preferred to worship the Canaanite precipitation deity known as Baal, and they institutionalized Baal-worship as the creed of the land. But then came Elijah, who posed an action-packed challenge to the cult of Baal. He called for 450 prophets of Baal (or, as they preferred to be known, "Major Baalers") to meet him atop Mount Carmel. There, Elijah and the Baal-boys each built altars and offered up sacrifices to their respective "gods." Elijah proclaimed that the winning deity would be the one that sent fire from the sky to burn up and consume the sacrifice.

Since the story is enshrined in the Tanakh, I think you can guess who won.

After this epic bull-burning smackdown, Elijah entered Jewish immortality, literally and figuratively. Elijah did not physically die—he was taken up directly by God in a whirlwind. And at the Passover Seder every year, we leave out a glass of wine for Elijah, believing that he visits every Jewish home. It seems like a lot of wine for one man to consume in one evening, but then again, he can always just get a ride home with his "Designated Whirlwind."

And according to the rabbis, Elijah will return to Earth to herald the messianic End of Days, at which time it is said he will settle all the arguments between Jews.

Forget prophet—if he wants to take that on, this guy's a *saint*!

THE ROCK STAR DOCUMENTARY

KING DAVID (c.1000 BCE) was the second ruler of the united ancient kingdom of Israel and Judah and a major expander of Israel's territory and power in the region.

But before all that, he had to find his voice.

David's other claim to fame is as the singer-songwriter behind many of "The Psalms," a timeless collection of poems, prayers, and songs canonized as a book of the Bible—so you *know* they're hardcore.

David was born to Jesse of Bethlehem, and as the youngest of eight sons, he felt the burning need to *make some noise.* Starting out as a shepherd, this tuneful tyke would pick up the harp and start shredding, serenading his woolly buddies with earworm ditties like "Stop Getting Eaten By Wolves" "(I Said) Stay Inside The Fence!" and "Seriously, Do You *Want* To Get Eaten?"

Then one day, a brash new act came to town.

Goliath, a giant sent by the Israelites' perpetual enemies the Philistines, challenged David's people to send out their best warrior to face him. For forty days, none dared to take on Big G.

That's when young David stepped out of the shadows, picked up a slingshot, and brought down Goliath with a single shot to the forehead. In other words...

Our future superstar had learned firsthand the power of rock.

And his powerful performance caught the eye of Israel's top promoter/monarch, King Saul. Saul sent David out into the battlefield as one of his top hitmakers, always able to win over a crowd (of angry Philistines, usually by killing them).

But for this rising star, success came at a price.

Before long, David was topping Saul in the charts—while Saul's popularity was falling. The critics (specifically the prophet Samuel, who chastised Saul for seeking personal gain over following God's laws) were brutal, and Saul became jealous of this young upstart waiting in the wings to "take over his residency at the palace."

So, Saul tried to have David killed, forcing this solo act to go out on the road before he even had an album to promote.

By this point, though, God had become a David superfan. When Saul died on the battlefield, David officially went gold (crown). Under their new frontman, David & The Israelites took Jerusalem by storm and made it the young nation's capital. However, even though Jerusalem was to one day hold the Holy Temple, David was banned from building it. His own critic, the prophet Nathan, told him it was prophesied that David's son would be the one to do so.

Like any celebrity contemplating his advancing age, David's first thought was, "So my kid can just get a jump-start right in the business? Cool."

And that's when love struck this legend down in his prime.

You see, one day while up on the palace roof (no doubt working out some "face-melting" harp progressions), David spotted a woman sunning herself. He fell hard for this bathing beauty, somehow trans-linguistically appropriately named "Bathsheba."

Problem is, she was already married.

And here David crossed the final threshold of all rock-and-roll immortals:

Destroying someone else's marriage.

He ordered Bathsheba's husband Uriah to be sent out to battle, to the front—where poor Uriah faced an "unscheduled tour cancellation."

Despite already having a wife (Michal, daughter of Saul—showbiz families, am I right?) and countless groupies, David married Bathsheba. And then, in classic *A Star is Born* fashion, he faced a new challenge on the scene from his own son, Absalom. Absalom led a rebellion against his old man but was defeated when his lustrous young-rocker-in-the-making long hair got caught in a tree.

David greatly mourned his fallen son, but—despite another challenge from another son, Adonijah—still managed to put his and Bathsheba's son, Solomon, on the throne. And, according to Isaiah, David's bloodline is the one that will one day give rise to the Messiah.

So next time you hear one of David's psalms in synagogue or church, raise a lighter to the ever-rocking memory of Old King D. Maybe even make a little donation.

Because like most artists past and present, even after 3,000 years, he still hasn't seen a penny in royalties.

A REAL WISE GUY

SOME PEOPLE SAY, "IT'S GOOD to be the king." But I tell you, it's a lot harder than it looks.

First of all, I got the gig when I was just a teenager! Oh, what's that, Israelites? You want me to control the lands from "from the Sea of Reeds to the Sea of the Philistines and from the desert to the Euphrates River?" Howzabout I start with *my hormones*?

It's also no picnic being a specifically Jewish king. You know why? Because we're always assigned a prophet to keep us in line. And by "prophet" I mean "Captain Buzzkill." *Thou shalt not* this, *thou shalt not* that. The only way I got out from under my (and my old man's) prophet Nathan's thumb was to point to something far away and say, "Hey, look over there—it's a vision from the Lord!"

Also, my old man, King David, majorly expanded the territory of Israel, which meant a huge expansion of trade routes. Great. So now every day it's like, "Sire, this delegation from the Kingdom of Whateveria wishes to trade you sixteen falcon livers for seven pieces of topaz. Will you trade?" And I'm like, sure, because call me what you will, I am *no topaz-hoarder*.

Except soon I kinda was, because all this trading was making me super rich. Which meant my boys from the old neighborhood said I was losing touch and no longer staying grounded. Even though I went out of my way to hang out with them, wearing my crown backwards at a rakish angle and saying, "Just call me S-Dog."

Then there was The Temple. Sure, you folks have your choice of which temple to go to (or to never set foot in). Me? I had to *frigging build my own*. Thanks, Dad, for leaving that one on my plate! And also, it kinda had to be THE Temple—like, the one God was going to personally hang out in, along with the Ark containing the Ten Commandments and the holy altar. No pressure there, S-Dog!

Still, I did it, and not gonna lie—it was a hit. Everyone who was (Jewishly) everyone was lining up at this thing multiple times a day, and pilgrims streamed in to see it from across the whole nation three times a year. Sacrificing bulls, oxen, goats, birds, you name it. Blood, smoke, and feathers 24/7.

In other words, *insane* clean-up bills!

But what people mostly say about me is, "That man was *wise!*" Which is true. I jotted down tons of sayings called "Proverbs," which made it into the Bible. I wrote a bunch of doom and gloom called "Ecclesiastes," which may still be the only poetry in history that is part of a book that people actually buy. I even snuck in a whole work of erotica called "Song of Solomon" into the same book that all those "thou shalt nots" came out of!

People came from near and far to experience my wisdom. The Queen of Sheba travelled all the way from Ethiopia to hang with me, and we really hit it off...right up until she found out about my 700 wives.

And the most famous story, you may have heard, was when two women came before me, each claiming that a baby was theirs. Here's how I solved that legendary conundrum:

WOMAN 1: This is my baby!

WOMAN 2: No, it's my baby!

SOLOMON: We shall slice the baby in half, and you can each have one slice.

WOMAN 1: Cool.

WOMAN 2: What? Slice my *baby*? Let her have it rather than that.

SOLOMON: Aha! The one who cares? *That's* the real mom! I am Solomon the Wise.

But what's less well-known is that was my response to *every* dispute. For example:

FARMER 1: This wheat field belongs to me!

FARMER 2: No, it belongs to me!

SOLOMON: We shall burn the field down, reducing the number of fields in dispute from one to *zero*.

FARMERS 1 AND 2: No wait! We can split it up. You don't have to—

SOLOMON: Too late! My people move fast. I am Solomon the Wise.

Or who could forget this adjudication?

PRIEST: This man cannot bring a sheep to sacrifice in the Holy Temple for he is impure.

MAN: But I just purified myself in the river!

SOLOMON: We shall clog the river, destroy the Temple, and use its stones to kill off every single sheep in Israel! I am Solomon the Wise.

PRIEST AND MAN: Do you…need to talk to someone?

Eventually, people stopped coming to me with their disputes. That, or the whole country ran out of things to burn, hack, slice, and destroy. Either way, I finally got some peace and quiet.

Now that's what I call "wisdom."

THE EXILE FILES

REHOBOAM
KING
ISRAEL, 10TH CENTURY BCE

Hi, it's me, Rehoboam, son of King Solomon. I know, I know, *Solomon the Wise, Solomon the Great.* How do you think it feels to be *Rehoboam the Random Offspring Of One Of Dad's 700 Wives*? But fortunately, even though my mom was an Ammonite (one of those "foreign women" God warned Dad to not get romantically involved with—bit of a micromanager aren't we, Big Guy?), I was the one he chose to take the throne after him.

But what he neglected to tell me about was the bill.

You see, Old King Sol famously built the most extravagant Temple you can imagine. Which was not cheap. So not cheap that it left our kingdom severely in debt. Meaning, it was up to *Rehoboam the Accounts Payable* to make up the shortfall. So, I levied this little itty-bitty tax on the Israelites. And the ten tribes of the North did not like that.

And they revolted, led by their own king, Jeroboam (or as I called him "The Lesser 'Boam"), broke off, and split the nation of twelve tribes into:

- Israel, made up of the ten tribes in the North,
- and Judah, made up of the two remaining tribes in the South, where the capitol Jerusalem was based.

Fortunately, this would be the last thing ever to divide the Jewish people.

JEREMIAH
PROPHET
JUDAH (A.K.A. THE SOUTHERN KINGDOM),
7TH CENTURY BCE

The thing about splintering a once-mighty nation in half? It turns it into two less-mighty-looking pieces. And this can suddenly look *very* appealing to any aspiring empires in the vicinity.

That's how the Babylonian Empire felt about Judah during my time. My prophecy-senses told me the Babylonians were going to attack us. And that we were going to lose. Grotesquely. Prophecies are *fun*!

Still, I put aside the temptation to make a killing on this information at the Illegal Sports-Betting Tent and instead brought my ominous report to King Zedekiah. Not my favorite conversation. "So, your Majesty, I've got some good news and some bad news…" (The good news was the discovery of a new kind of chickpea, which didn't really help cushion the blow.)

Even more difficult was my call to action to the King: "We should surrender. And after we've endured our punishment and made penance, God will consider restoring us to our land, *maybe*."

Well, you can imagine how popular that made me. Let's just say there's a reason I came to be voted "Prophet Most Often Imprisoned By The King." And it wasn't for my sports betting.

EZEKIEL
PROPHET
BABYLONIA, 6TH CENTURY BCE

Jerry nailed it! Jerusalem was indeed conquered by Babylon, which is where we were during my time. And it was a sad time. Led by Nebuchadnezzar, the Babylonians destroyed our Temple, took us out of the Promised Land, and made us into slaves again. It was like a total rewind of our history. I half-expected us to spend forty years in the desert walking backwards and vomiting up manna.

This exile is what people famously have described with the phrase "by the waters of Babylon," indicating the riverbanks where we sat around, mourning our lost land. Wisely, though, we moved our national existential collective wailing to higher ground during heavy rains.

On the more hopeful side, I had a vision featuring a valley full of "dry bones" coming back to life, which was supposedly a metaphor for our resurrection as a nation. I didn't manage to delve any deeper, because people tune you out when you begin conversations with "I had the craziest dream…"

However, that one was tame compared to the other vision I saw while in Babylon. This one featured the spirit of God, also leaving the Promised Land behind and coming to join us in our sad river-adjacent tears. This was a moving and radically new Jewish idea: When humans are suffering, God shows up to join them in their grief. Often sheepishly holding a tray of slightly burned homemade lasagna.

But the theology wasn't the craziest part: It was the imagery. In this vision, I saw God's presence as a mystical sky chariot, driven by amazing creatures who each had four faces: that of a man, lion, ox, and eagle. And this chariot ran on "wheels within wheels," each of which were themselves filled with the eyes of God.

This set of images later became a major source of inspiration for the Kabbalists (see p. 112), but yeah, I was definitely not bringing up this dream at the office.

EZRA
PRIEST/SCRIBE
ISRAEL, 5TH CENTURY BCE

We're back, baby! Turns out the Babylonians got conquered by the Persians. And their accurately-named king, "Cyrus the Great," let the Jews return to Israel and rebuild the Temple after fifty years. This was the fastest any project in history would ever get finished by Israeli contractors.

And this time, they added so much more opulence and magnificence, some suspected we were just trying to flip the Temple for a potential future buyer. But I knew it takes a lot more than a fancy building to hold a recently scattered people together. I thought: *How about giving them a common enemy?* Then I remembered we already had like nine of those and it hadn't helped.

So I tried another tack: giving them a *shared history*. I wrote down a lot of what had happened to us in the books of Chronicles, Nehemiah, Malachi, and my own self-titled release, Ezra. (I also wrote a series of mystery scrolls following the adventures of a Detective Methuselah Jones, but those don't seem to have met the test of time.)

Beyond that, we needed structure. So I came up with these innovations:

1) Weekly public readings aloud from the Torah. Although sadly, few readers listened to my repeated pleas to "Do the voices!"

2) The Amidah, the prayer done while standing that's central to Jewish worship. As well as the livelihoods of countless chiropractors and cobblers.

3) The Sanhedrin, the main legislative body of BCE Israel. Imagine the US Congress, but somehow even more ancient-looking and Bible-obsessed.

And finally, I came up with the annual holiday of Purim. But I'll leave that tale to my colleague…

ESTHER
QUEEN
PERSIA, 5TH CENTURY BCE

So, funny story: Despite Cyrus' decree, not all of us actually ended up going back to the homeland. Some of us had a pretty good thing going in the Diaspora and stuck around in the Persian Empire. That's where I lived with my uncle/cousin/genealogy unclear, Mordechai.

Then along came Cyrus' descendant, King Ahasuerus. And he was looking for a new queen. So he announced a competition of sorts, extending an invitation to any and every unmarried woman across the 127 provinces of the Persian Empire. Talk about having a type!

Mordechai persuaded me to hide the fact that I was Jewish and try out…and I got the gig! My uncle/cousin was relieved because I would be set up for life and he could finally stop setting me up on catastrophic blind dates.

But one day, King Ahasuerus appointed an adviser named Haman whose only advice seemed to be, "Hey, how about we kill all the Jews?" Which, on top of being bloodthirsty and bigoted, is *such* a cliché!

Still, Haman got the king to issue his decree, and there was only one person who could speak up against it: the queen. Who, remember, the king did not know was Jewish. Which had made things really hard to explain every year when he was attending my family's Seder.

I was terrified to speak up, but finally Mordechai told me that perhaps all these bizarre twists and turns had brought me to this place and time. He said that being the secretly Jewish Queen of Persia just as the Persian army threatened the Jews was part of a higher plan. Or at least an enormously entertaining soap opera.

So I threw a bunch of banquets, and chose just the right moment to let the king know that his advice-guy was about to advise him into sleeping alone. (I mean, if you don't count his concubines, but between you and me, most of them snored.)

And long megillah short: It worked! Haman was executed, the Jews were saved, and I decreed that we eternally dishonor the memory of Haman by eating cookies shaped like his ears.

In other words, food won. Now *that's* what I call a Jewish victory!

THE WOMEN'S SECTION

THE PLACE OF WOMEN IN Jewish history can best be described in one word: *complicated*. As with many traditional religions and cultures, they are somehow both marginalized and central. Which is not surprising considering how most women can accomplish two or more things at the same time.

Naturally, the story begins with the first woman, **Eve**. However, unlike in Christianity, Jewish tradition does not blame Eve for humanity's downfall and inherent sinfulness. Instead, she and Adam get full and equal billing for breaking God's Very First Rule. You go, girl!

From there on in the Hebrew Bible, women pop up with much less frequency than men but often with pivotal roles. There are, of course, the matriarchs: **Sarah, Rebecca, Rachel, and Leah.** Although largely restricted to being bearers (or often frustrated not-yet-bearers) of children to carry on the Jewish legacy, they each tackled this goal in very different ways. Sarah laughs at God when God says she'll get pregnant in her nineties. Rebecca deceives her dying husband to make sure the "Jewier" son gets the spiritual inheritance. And Rachel and Leah (and their conveniently fertile handmaidens) engage in an epic arms race for the title of World's Busiest Womb.

Women are foundational to the Exodus story. After Pharaoh enslaves the Hebrews and decrees that all Jewish baby boys be killed (#sexist), it takes five Jewish women to save Moses:

- the midwives Shifra and Puah, who defy Pharaoh's order and keep the babies alive (because the alternative would likely take a toll on their "midwife word-of-mouth")

- the daughter of Pharaoh, who rescues the baby from the floating crib he was placed in the Nile (history's first example of a Jewish mother worrying about her son experiencing too much humidity)

- Moses' sister Miriam, who makes sure he's nursed by his mother, Yocheved (also sparing a lactating Yocheved the embarrassment of Nile-side "pump and dumps")

Miriam goes on to play a supporting role in the actual Exodus, leading songs of celebration and, according to the Rabbis, being the mystical provider of water in the desert. So in addition to being a prophetess (see below), Miriam's key roles as song leader and hydrator-in-chief would have definitely qualified her to run Jewish summer camps.

Other smaller yet often crucial roles were played by women throughout the Tanakh. There are different accounts, but at least seven women were considered by all to be prophets (see p. 45):

- Sarah, the Matriarch

- Miriam

- Deborah, the Judge (see p. 40 and above about women doing two things at once)

- Hannah, considered the originator of spontaneous individual prayer
- Abigail, one of King David's "early" wives
- Huldah, a coworker of Jeremiah
- Queen Esther

The daughters of **Zelophehad (Mahlah, Noa, Hoglah, Milcah,** and **Tirzah)** are five women who were done wrong by tribal inheritance laws. So they protested to Moses and actually got God to change His Divine Mind so they could inherit their father's property. It's pretty wild that, among the Israelites, it was women who had the biggest *cojones*.

Abigail and **Michal** both married King David at different times, and were active behind the throne, although sadly none of them ever rode around on Jewish dragons. And again, Queen Esther got her own book and famously saved the Jewish people's (inability to eat) bacon.

In some aspects, the Torah puts women and men on equal footing. It specifies that both Israelite men and women were present at the giving of the Torah at Sinai and were required to make sacred pilgrimage to the Temple in Jerusalem for the three main festivals: Pesach, Shavuot, and Sukkot—although only the men refused to stop and ask for directions.

But the bulk of the Torah's hundreds of commandments were binding only for men. Women were exempt from things like having to pray three times a day at different times of the day and having to buy palm fronds, myrtles, willows, and a surprisingly expensive citrus fruit for Sukkot. The historical record shows zero complaints.

In later generations, the all-male rabbis sometimes bordered on obsession with legislating women's bodies and choices (a shocking departure from the modern world). There's an entire book of the Talmud, for instance, devoted to laws around menstruation and ritual purity. I do not recommend reading it before lunch.

The general principle the rabbis settled on was that women—already fully scheduled taking care of spouse and children—are not obligated by commandments that have to be performed at a certain time (like hearing the shofar play on Rosh Hashanah). The three essentials were: lighting Shabbat candles, preparing the challah, and maintaining the above-mentioned menstrual purity. (*Obsessed*, I'm telling you!)

That said, women were educated in Jewish law throughout the Bible, and this was considered a plus for marriageability. The Talmud relates many stories of Jewish women who lost their husbands but continued their children's education. However, the Talmud is silent regarding how these single homeschooling moms handled prom.

Among them were **Beruriah,** wife of Rabbi Meir; **Yalta,** wife of Rabbi Nachman, and **Imma Shalom,** the wife of Eliezer ben Hyrcanus. **Rachel** inspired her husband Akiva to give up shepherding at age forty and become one of the greatest sages of all time—a definite upgrade in career and "day-to-day workplace odor."

In the Middle Ages, women made incremental progress in what functions they were permitted to participate in, but they were still banned from most professions like all Jews in Christian and Muslim societies (see p. 97). Essentially, they earned only 70 percent of what their husbands were not allowed to make.

But more and more women sought out education, participated in public Jewish practices, and even formed prayer groups. Unfortunately, there's no sign that these groups adopted cheeky women's-bowling-league-style names like "Shebrew" or "The Siddur Sisters."

In subsequent centuries, Jewish women attained slightly higher status. Some helped their husbands in business or ran their own. Some lent money to Christian women in Europe, and some worked as copyists, spinners, and weavers (preferably not simultaneously). Still, they faced multiple limitations. Women could not attend yeshivot (seminary) and become clergy. They were required to pray in a segregated section (lest their feminine charms—including their voices and general existence—distract men from prayer). And their wardrobe and hair was subject to strictures of "modesty," that is, keeping it covered. (Not that Jewish men were exactly strutting around flexing their yeshiva-untanned abs either.)

Crucially, they could not obtain a divorce unless their husbands initiated it. In other words, women already trapped in miserable marriages were also placed in the historically excruciating position of "Waiting on a dude to get off his tuchus."

This last issue (male divorce-control, not tuchuses) continues to be a challenge for Jewish women in the Orthodox movement to this day. As Europe passed through the Enlightenment into the modern era and more liberal branches of Judaism emerged (see p. 133), the status of women became one of the main points of difference between denominations. That and the never-ending simmering competition as to which movement's synagogues can put out the most unhealthy kiddush.

Today, Orthodoxy continues to regard women in a similar vein, although some branches have diverged. In 2010, **Sara**

Hurwitz was named an Orthodox "Rabba," or female rabbi, and cofounded the New York–based yeshiva Maharat, the first institution to ordain Orthodox women as clergy. Which is proof that you really *can* get anything in New York.

By contrast, the Reform movement—which, as we shall see later, refutes the authority of Jewish law as traditionally interpreted—maintains full equality in every sphere for women. Yes, even including peeing their name in the snow.

The Reconstructionist movement has made this a founding principle. Conservative Judaism has, as always, hewed a middle path—but the upshot is the same. In all three non-Orthodox movements, you will find examples of sisters "Jewing it for themselves."

The modern state of Israel has favored more egalitarian female participation, particularly when more hands have been needed to work on kibbutzim and fight enemy nations. In fact, in 1969, Israel elected a female Prime Minister, **Golda Meir,** while the United States and many Western nations have still failed to do so. (Elect a female leader that is, not elect Golda Meir, which—since she's been dead for half a century—would make her the first Jewish Woman Zombie leader.)

Jewish women around the world have risen to prominence in every field, from medicine to media to business to politics, although some sadly feel the need to downplay this around fragile men on their dating profiles. We'll see more examples later, but **Barbra Streisand** is one of the world's most beloved entertainers. Cosmetic guru **Estée Lauder**'s achievements continue to literally be on the lips of millions. The late **Ruth Bader Ginsburg** was a leading champion of civil rights on the US Supreme Court in between her day job as "fashion influencer." **Sheryl Sandberg** is one of the founders of

Facebook, still the world's number one cause of lost workplace productivity.

Today's Jewish women are leaders, channeling the power of their biblical matriarchy toward taking on and quashing the patriarchy—while raising families, supporting partners, and balancing their own professions and sanity. Still, they have a long way to go to reach parity with men. However, nowadays this is less due to specifically Jewish factors than to the continuing prevalent "men are pigs" factor. Yes, even the kosher ones.

SO THEN...

THAT HAPPENED

THE MARKETING MEETING

INT. JERUSALEM—168 BCE—DAY

MATTATHIAS: OK, roll call! Are all my sons here? Judah, Eleazar, Simon, John, and Jonathan?

THE BROTHERS: Present!

MATTATHIAS: Well, as the head priest of the ruling Hasmonean dynasty of occupied Judea—I should really put that on a business card—I've called you all here for a reason: The Jewish people are in trouble!

A collective gasp.

SIMON: You mean because our land is a colonized pawn, caught in the crossfire of Egypt's Ptolemaic Empire, and Syria's Seleucid Empire?

JOHN: Because the new emperor Antiochus desecrated our holy Temple, forced us to eat pork, and made it a crime for the Jewish people to get circumcised?

JONATHAN: Like anyone could tell if *you* got snipped or not.

JOHN: Shut up, *Mr. Three-Syllables*!

MATTATHIAS: As I was saying, the fate of the Jewish people hangs in the balance because…we're running out of popularity!

Awkward beat.

ELEAZAR: Might I suggest we'd be more popular if we were cool with eating pork and not cutting off our—

MATTATHIAS: Now as a priest, I happen to be privy to certain…future revelations. One day, many thousands of years from now, we Jews shall live under the control of another nation.

JOHN: What else is new?

MATTATHIAS: And that nation and its brethren shall worship another god.

JONATHAN: Lemme guess: The moon? A giant statue? A three-toed sloth?

MATTATHIAS: Actually, one of our own. A carpenter from Nazareth who…got a pretty big promotion.

SIMON: To what? *Head* carpenter? Carpenter in Chief? Assistant Regional Manager for Carpentry?

MATTATHIAS: Not exactly: To *god*.

The Hasmonean boys gape at their father, confused.

MATTATHIAS: Many other big nations will also come to worship this god. And they will hold a sacred feast to honor his birthday. A feast so important, they will begin decorations for it months in advance, seemingly earlier and earlier each year. So important, they will build entire businesses—even towns—around it. So important, they will give it their culture's highest honor: a series of cheesy love stories on something called "cable television."

ELEAZAR: Hey, I got the answer, Pops: How about we Hasmonean brothers gather our forces and *destroy all birthdays*!

MATTATHIAS: Well, Eleazar, you're not far off from what I'm thinking. But first, we must gather our forces and drive the Seleucid Empire out of our land!

JUDAH: Brilliant! By breaking King Antiochus' shackles, we will show peoples everywhere that the pure in heart can overcome even the mightiest of foes! We shall call ourselves... *(loooong dramatic pause)* THE MACCABEES!

MATTATHIAS: That's nice, son. But it's beside the point. We have to keep our eyes on the main goal: *Creating a holiday that blows Carpenter Boy's b-day out of the water!*

The brothers look at each other, confused.

JUDAH: But we're...still going to drive the Seleucid Empire out of our land?

MATTATHIAS: Oh totally! And it will involve a miracle that people shall speak of for centuries!

SIMON: The miracle of defeating a vastly superior army?

MATTATHIAS: No! The miracle of not having enough pure olive oil to light the menorah in our Sacred Temple. And then, right after that...wait for it...*having enough oil!*

ELEAZAR: Uh…

MATTATHIAS: What part of "not having oil then suddenly having oil" doesn't scream "miracle" at you? This is the Middle East—entire nations rise and fall based on oil supplies!

JOHN: Pop…I'm still a little lost on how exactly we'll ruin the Carpenter-God's birthday? Are we going to, like, make him go to work that day? Have his annoying little sibling's birthday occur the same week?

MATTATHIAS: It's not so much that we're going to ruin this day of "Christmas"—it's that our holiday is going to blow *his* out of the water!

JUDAH: I still think beating an entire imperial army already seems pretty miraculous…

MATTATHIAS: Oh yeah? Well sounds like you lack imagination! Picture this, boys.

Mattathias gets up, uses his arms to make the sales presentation of his life.

MATTATHIAS: Jews everywhere lighting their own tiny menorahs—not grand and golden like the one in the Temple, but cruddy with wax. And get this: We'll do this for *eight days straight! Eight times as many days as the birthday boy gets!*

ELEAZAR: So that's it? We'll light lamps in our homes for just slightly over a week?

MATTATHIAS: Oh, I'm just getting started. Our voices will also rise in glorious song—well, one or two songs that no one quite remembers every verse to. Businesses will feature a tiny picture of this menorah that you can *almost* make out amidst the Christmas decorations! And children will eagerly look forward to this day all year round, when we honor it by giving them presents that can be obtained in drug stores for small amounts of money!

JUDAH: And this will, once and for all, wipe out the not-yet-existing existential threat to the Jewish people known as "Christmas"?

MATTATHIAS: Nah. But at least it's something to do in the depressing month we will one day call "December."

FROM ROMANS
TO ROAMERS

From 63 BCE to 132 CE, the last in the series of great powers to occupy the Holy Land was the Roman Empire. They would discover, just as the Egyptians, Assyrians, Babylonians, Persians, and Seleucids had, that these particular subjects seemed to have a special allergy to conquest.[1]

Not helping Rome either was the fact that this land, which they called "Judea," was being torn apart by four Jewish factions:

o The Sadducees: The priestly class who offered the sacrifices at the Temple but sometimes succumbed to the corruptions of the job. To be fair, can anyone resist the temptations of fresh-burned turtledove?

o The Pharisees: The working-class teachers of our traditions, and precursors to today's rabbis.[2]

o The Zealots: The militant revolutionaries, constantly amped up to fight Roman authority—especially after they came home from their first semester of college.

---

1   Ironic for a people who often have trouble conquering allergies.
2   The term still has a pejorative association to this day. This is because in the New Testament, the Pharisees were Jesus' adversaries—most notably when they faced him in hand-to-hand combat in "Jesus-dome."

- ○ The Essenes: The mystics who retreated to caves in the desert to meditate—at least until the other three "stopped the yelling!"

Into this raucous squabble entered a very "unconventional" Jew named Jesus of Nazareth (see p. 199). To do this figure justice would take another book (or, really, twenty-seven). But suffice it to say: To the Jews, Jesus was a radical religious reformer. To the Romans, he was a dangerous political rebel. And to everyone else, an incredibly concise way to say, "I just stubbed my toe!" or "This phone bill's too high!"

The rise of Jesus and his followers, the Christian apostles, coincided with the rise of Zealot-style military resistance to Rome. Over the decades, Roman authorities had gotten more and more heavy-handed in their efforts to wipe out Judaism and Jewish practice. They sought to replace them with Roman ways. The infamously hedonistic emperor Caligula was said by the Jewish historian Philo to have "regarded the Jews with especial suspicion,"[3] which is pretty rich coming from a guy who reportedly slept with his sisters and appointed his horse to public office.

But Caligula pushed things too far when he had a statue of himself placed in the Temple in Jerusalem. This violated the Jewish people's "red line" against idolatry and sacrilege. Fed up and out of patience, the Jews launched a rebellion in 66 CE, which ended in 73 CE. Now ruled by Emperor Titus, Rome besieged and smashed through the walls of Jerusalem, and their army burned the Temple to the ground. So you could say this rebellion was not a "success."

---

3   Philo, *The Works of Philo Judaeus*, Ch. 16 https://en.wikisource.org/wiki/
The_Works_of_Philo_Judaeus/On_the_Embassy_to_Gaius#XVI

From 115–117 CE, Jews in diaspora communities like Cyprus, Mesopotamia, and Egypt also rose up in rebellion against Roman oppression. Either that, or they *really* hated being forced to learn Latin.

Then, in 132 CE, a third and final uprising took place, led by a man named Shimon Bar-Kokhba. Bar-Kokhba was hailed at the time as the "Jewish Messiah" by one of Judaism's greatest scholars/late-bloomers, Rabbi Akiva (see p. 67 [Rachel/Women's Section])

Despite this celebrity endorsement, Bar-Kokhba and his ilk only managed to wrest a little breathing room from the Romans for three years. Their final showdown took place atop the fortress of Masada, where the last Jewish holdouts chose to take their own lives rather than become Roman slaves. Today, their courage is honored by Israel Defense Forces recruits swearing allegiance atop Masada and legions of tourists bravely adorning it with abandoned soda bottles.

But back in that era, Rome decided to just get rid of the pesky Judeans once and for all. They demolished Jerusalem and kicked the Jewish people out of it.

And so, driven from their holy city and capitol, a multitude of the Jewish people left the Promised Land and got back to one of their top core competencies: wandering.

Rome's Arch of Titus commemorates Emperor Titus's conquest of Jerusalem. Even to this day, as a point of honor, Jewish visitors to Rome refuse to pass beneath it.

PART 2

....

DHU NUWAS
WARLORD
YEMEN, 6TH CENTURY CE

OK, so win some, lose some—or in this case, lose an entire national homeland. No matter. After the failure of the Bar-Kokhba revolt, Roman oppression got so bad, we Jews began spreading out across the globe. And a lot of us ended up in Yemen. In fact, we started the first functional Jewish state since Judea. This is well-documented because a fourth century Christian missionary to the region named Theophilos complained that there were "too many Jews around." Hey, Theo, leave the complaining to the professionals!

During my time, Yemen (like most places) was less a country and more an agglomeration of tribes. I was the chief of a Jewish tribe, and we often got into territorial battles with others. But to keep things clear, I was given the nickname *Dhu Nuwas*, as in "Lord Sidelocks"—as in those long curly hairlocks that some religious Jewish men let their facial hair grow out into. For an ethnically identifying battle name, it still beats "The Fighting Foreskinless."

But they sure didn't call me that "Sidelocks" nickname mockingly. Because I was a fearsome warlord who united several battling tribes, fought off an invasion, and may have, um, kind of massacred thousands of Christians who refused to join my tribe.

Still got something to say about my facial hair, punk?

DIHYA AL-KAHINA
SORCERESS
NORTH AFRICA, 7TH CENTURY CE

After Rome made us want to leave Judea, some Jews went east like those Yemenites, but others went west. My cohorts and I spread into northwest Africa or the Maghreb, settling in whatever pockets of tolerance would have us (until they learned that we don't do alterations on Saturday).

One of those welcoming groups was called the Berbers. You may be familiar with Berber carpets—shaggy and rough-hewn with long loops, beloved by home decorators, reviled by home cleaners. Well, the Berbers not only took us Jews in, some of them even became Jewish themselves! I mean, we've all heard of Arabic hospitality, but there's such a thing as *trying too hard*, guys.

As for me, I rose to power as a military leader in an area around the Aures Mountains and fought to keep my turf—as well as my fellow Jews—free from the encroaching Muslim conquest of the region. And according to legend, one of the secrets to my military success was magical powers.

I'll neither confirm nor deny this. But let's just say, no rival warring tribe chose to stick around after I strode into battle, marched up to their chieftain, looked him dead in the eye and whispered, "Pick a card, any card."

BULAN
KING
KHAZARIA, 8TH CENTURY CE

I became king of a Turkic region called Khazaria, wedged in between Europe, the Baltics, and the Arabian lands. But unlike most places on both the Europe and Arabia side, my people didn't have an official state religion. I wanted to choose one, but first, I wanted to do some comparison shopping.

So I brought in a Muslim, Christian, and Jew to hold a debate on whose faith was superior—or as I called it, "My God Can Beat Up Your God." I was so impressed with the Jew, I decided to convert myself and my whole kingdom to Judaism.

My decision ended one debate—but launched thousands more. Centuries later, some conspiracy-mongers still claim that all Ashkenazic (European) Jews are actually descended from these "fake Jews," and therefore Judaism has no authentic lineage, and Jews have no historical connection to the land of Israel.

Even though scholars have repeatedly destroyed this claim, at least we know the valuable significance of the term "Khazar Jew." As soon as you hear someone spouting it, that means it's time to leave the party.

HIWI AL-BALKHI
SKEPTIC
AFGHANISTAN, 9TH CENTURY CE

Some say Afghan Jews date back to the original "lost" ten tribes of Northern Israel, separated from Judah and Ephraim during Rehoboam and Jeroboam's "great divorce" almost a millennium ago. Or maybe those tribes knew exactly where they were but were just trying to get away from overbearing Jewish parents.

In any case, merchant routes like the Silk Road brought Jews through this area for centuries, until eventually some of us said, "Enough merchanting—I'm staying!"

By my time, the Jewish community in Afghanistan was so well-established, it even had room for me: a skeptical scholar of Jewish texts. In my most famous work, I outlined 200 objections to the idea of the Bible being written by God. Only later did I finally hit upon Incontestable Proof #201 that God wouldn't have written it: too much "sex stuff."

Still, my book was so provocative, it inspired an entire book of rebuttal written by the famous scholar Saadia Gaon, who's name literally means "Saadia the Genius."

So call me "Hiwi al-Balkhi" no more. From now on, it's "Hiwi, Irritator of Geniuses!"

BENJAMIN OF TUDELA
EXPLORER
SAMARKAND, UZBEKISTAN, 12TH CENTURY CE

I'm originally from Tudela, Spain. But like many contemporaries, I spent my life away from Spain, exploring the world outside. In fact, a lot of Spanish Jews of this age spent their time getting away from Spain. At some point should Spain take this personally? Maybe do a quick armpit check?

During my travels, I visited about three hundred cities across Europe, Asia, and the Middle East. Some even called me the "Jewish Marco Polo." Which makes me all the more angry that no one plays a game yelling my name out in swimming pools.

One of the more far-flung sites of Jewish habitation I found was in Samarkand, in deepest Central Asia, between Russia and China and Japan. Here dwelled a Jewish community combining Sephardic, Persian, and Turkic traditions, and they called themselves "Bukharans." Which is much a nicer-sounding Jewish name than "mutts."

The Bukharans would come to live under the rule of many empires: the Mongols under Genghis and Kublai Khan, the Timurid Empire under Tamerlane the Great, and the Soviet Union all the way from Lenin through Gorbachev. Each time one of them fell, the Bukharans would look at each other, shrug, and say, "Empire, shmempire. What's for dinner?"

But after the fall of the Soviets, most of the Bukharans would leave their one thousand-year-old traditional neighborhood and emigrate en masse to either Queens, New York, or Israel (the Queens of the Middle East).

Even more amazingly, even after a thousand years, they would get their deposit back.

COLLECT 'EM ALL!

So HOW DOES A PEOPLE hold onto a robust, already two thousand-year-old culture when they've moved far away from their land and sacred capitol?

Through one of the Jewish people's favorite things of all-time: *words.*

Rabbi Yochanan Ben Zakai was exiled by Rome, and he set the tone of the incredible transformation about to overtake Judaism. He argued that without a Temple to make daily sacrifices at, the Jews needed a replacement ritual. That became prayer, and people's local synagogues and temples became proxies for the central one in Jerusalem that now had a "No Jews Allowed—THIS MEANS YOU" sign taped over it.

Over the ensuing centuries, the rabbis took this idea even further, ruling that the three main pillars of Judaism would henceforth be: Torah study, prayer, and acts of kindness. (There were not quite enough votes for a proposed fourth pillar: "Shrugging.")

They would devote the next two thousand years to figuring out exactly how to do those three things, developing a series of collected works: the Mishnah, the Gemara (together forming The Talmud), the Midrash, and enough books of scriptural interpretation and legal analysis to give even Samson a hernia.

They were The Rabbis, and (in a society in which this status was not yet permitted to women) they were *Men of Action...*

Hillel

Ability — The Oralizer

Co-creating the Oral Law (the explanatory complement to Written Law) *with a mouth full of razor-sharp teeth*

Insight

Constantly locked in scholarly battle with his nemesis, Rabbi Shammai…*to the death* (of ignorance)

Rider

Leading the Jewish sages in elucidating the mysteries of Torah…*atop his fiery steed*

Code Name: "Big Mouth"   Location: Israel/Judaea

Yochanan ben Zakai

1st century CE

Ability **Sneakery**

Sneaking out of Rome-occupied Judea *disguised as a corpse* (seriously!)

Almost Famous

Getting a meeting with future Roman Emperor Vespasian *and his fist*

Tough Crowd

Establishing the first-ever center of Jewish learning *with no fundraising committee*

Code Name: "The Schoolmaster"   Location: Israel/Judea

Yehuda HaNasi

2nd century CE

Ability **Editing**

Writing down the Oral Law, Torah, and rabbinic wisdom, *with his bare hands*

Killer Quill

Editing all that into the Mishnah with his red editing pen, *which uses the blood of his enemies*

Big Arms

Using giant Mishnah volumes *to crush enemy skulls*

Code Name: "The Prince"   Location: Israel/Judea

Abayye and Rava
4th century CE
Ability
Stamina
Locked in centuries of mortal argumentation
Diggers
Unearthing the meaning of the Mishnah with their diamond-edged shovels
Flame Bearers
Set the tone of Talmudic dispute... one fiery proof at a time
Code Name: "The Dialectical Duo"
Location: Babylonia

Rashi

11th century CE

Ability — Mind Control

Elucidating every single sacred Jewish text...*using only his mind*

Time Agent

Commentaries still cited today *thanks to his time-travel powers*

Fontmaster

Creating his own font *by smashing other fonts to bits*

Code Name: "Frenchie"   Location: France

Yehuda HaLevi

Ability **Power Poetry**

Penning prayers and songs still in our prayerbooks...
which could totally give you a papercut!

Hearts and Minds

Instilling a love for Zion in Jewish hearts...*with his trusty
cardio-scythe!*

Wanderlust

Traveling to Jerusalem in the middle of the Crusades
— *what a badass!*

Code Name: "The Poet Warrior"   Location: Spain

Maimonides

12th century CE

Ability — Rationalizer

Writing *The Guide to the Perplexed*, ramming Torah into perplexed people's brains

Tzedakah-Master

Creating the Jewish "Eight Levels of Charity" — *and vanquishing the Boss on each*

Contritionizer

Teaching Jews the fundamentals of how to atone…*or face his blade*

Code Name: "Rambam"

Location: Egypt

Yosef Caro

16th century CE

Ability — Codifier

Codifying centuries of Jewish law with *one arm tied behind his back*

Team-Builder

Put together a law book with Rabbi Moshe Isserles, *in a no-holds-barred tag-team match*

Law Bearer

Literally *laid down the law, mofos*

Code Name: "Big Joe"

Location: Spain, Israel

THE JEWS' MIDDLE-AGES CRISIS

MAKE NO MISTAKE: THE CENTURIES after the fall of the Roman Empire were basically terrible for *everyone*. Europe was now dominated by Christianity and feudalism, a.k.a., "the fun duo." This meant that a tiny elite class kept most of the population in abject poverty. There was also constant warfare, just in case those peasants were getting too used to their sweet life of nothing. Education and literacy were practically nonexistent. And finally, the Bubonic Plague decimated a third of the population. No wonder people enjoy spending their weekends dressing up and reliving this magical period!

Likewise, the rise of Islam across the Arabian Peninsula sparked centuries of strife and disruption. Mini empires fought to fill in the power vacuum, and religious factions fought tooth and sandy nail over who had inherited the true faith.[1]

Unsurprisingly, for the Jews, things were even worse.

In both cases, the political rulers—from top to bottom—derived their political authority from the idea that they were appointed by God.[2] This meant they were given license,

---

1   Just think how many lives could have been spared by one good probate lawyer!

2   Along with their other main source of authority: a gang of beefy guys on horseback wielding swords.

although some would say *obligated*, to force everyone under their rule to worship as they did. As for those who didn't...

You can see where this is going. In both Europe and Arabia, Jews were relegated to second-class status. Or, more often, the status of number two. Jews were forced to live in designated areas and were not legally allowed to own property or practice most professions.[3] In Europe, Jews in the country were often restricted to the small villages or shtetls they lived in, while Jews in the city were forced to live in specified neighborhoods or ghettos. That's right, we invented *those* too!

PROPHET SHARING

Islam started in the 600s, several centuries after the Jews left Judea and got back to their beloved hobby of "refugeeing." This meant there were many Jewish communities and tribes spread out across the Arab world, poised to create eternal battles over who really invented hummus. Some of them fought with Muhammad's army as it established supremacy over the region. In 641, Muhammad's successor Caliph Umar issued a covenant affording protection to the Christians and Jews...but in kinda the same way that the Godfather offers "protection."

Over the centuries, many other caliphs came and went, and most of them permitted Jewish residency...provided the Jews stayed in their camel lane. You see, Islam had a designated category in its theology for the Jews: dhimmis, the "protected ones." This was because Muslims also trace their ancestry back to Abraham/Ibrahim (in other words, centuries of strife can be traced back to daddy issues). And they consider

---

3   On the plus side, *zero pressure from Jewish parents to go to law or med school.*

the Torah—and many of its leading figures like Moses and David—sacred.

All of which meant that Jews had a solid, guaranteed place in the Muslim hierarchy—it just needed to be below Islam's.

So in practice, Jews living in Arab lands got more freedom to study and practice their own religion. As long as they kept to their Jew-places, practiced only a handful of "acceptable" professions for a Jew, and kept quiet, they were largely left alone. Despite the enormous effort this required from Jews for the "keep quiet" part.

THE DARK AGES FINALLY TURN BAD

By contrast, the European Christians had no way to rationalize the continued *existence* of the Jews. In the theological redemption arc embodied by Jesus, Christianity was supposed to have replaced Judaism entirely. And yet, even long after Jesus's death and ascension, and despite the rise of Christianity around the globe, the Jews still...*were*. Medieval European Christians would have said, "Read the room!" except that 99.999 percent of them couldn't read.

Even worse, many believed the Jews killed Jesus. Which was, at best, awkward when it came up at parties. And at worst, even though Jesus's death had happened centuries earlier, many people held currently living Jews personally liable for it. That's right, the Jews—who invented the very concept of the "scapegoat" in the Torah (Leviticus 16:8)—got to be the first to test-drive it. Or strictly speaking, be test-driven out because of it.

And for Medieval Jews, this accusation took an even darker and more dangerous turn. In this deeply "pre-medical" time, when mortality was limited in general and child mortality was rampant, Jews were accused of murdering Christian children. Whenever disease broke out, Jews were blamed for having caused it by poisoning the wells. When a Christian child went missing, rumors circulated that the Jews had kidnapped and ritually slaughtered the child, using their blood to bake Passover matzo. This is literally impermissible in Judaism, as matzo has to be made without moisture and human blood is not kosher. However, medieval Christian peasants were not schooled in the fine points of Jewish law. Or, you know, just plain schooled.

THE CRUSADES: HISTORY'S WORST ROAD TRIP

Fortunately, European Christendom did not blame the Jews for *all* their woes. That's what the Muslims were for! Specifically, the ones rapidly taking over much of Arabia, Africa, and Asia—with a brand-new religion that essentially gave their guy Jesus a *demotion* to mere "prophet?"

Even worse, these "external infidels" (as opposed to the Jewish ones more conveniently close at hand) had taken over Jerusalem! Now I know what you're thinking: *Wasn't Jerusalem kinda the Jewish people's capital for hundreds of years?*

Yes! It was! But more recently, Jerusalem was also the backdrop to the New Testament's climactic chapters of Jesus's life, death, and resurrection. All those sites, plus others that had become enshrined into Jesus's final days, were now sacred to Christianity's story. For years, legions of Christian pilgrims had come to walk in the path of Jesus's last steps and reenact his final days. But with Muslims in control, that was no longer possible.

Now, Christianity is supposedly a religion that prizes forgiveness, but the one thing you do not mess with is their *role-playing games*.

So in 1095, Pope Urban II called upon a man named Peter the Hermit[4] to gather volunteer troops in Germany, go to Jerusalem, and fight to wrest the sacred city out of Muslim hands. Peter recruited thousands by creating a festive atmosphere, which included massacring Jews. He is rumored to have wanted to name this event "Burning Mensch." However, history gave it the pithier title, "The Crusades."

This first band of "Crusaders" marched for the Holy Land but got killed by Turkish warriors before they even arrived. Still, at least they died doing what they loved: hating.

But the Crusade concept had spread through Europe, like the Black Death if it was being run by white people. Soon various nations were sending their best and brightest—no wait, actually, their worst and dullest. They sent the sons who were too dumb to pursue higher studies, too unreliable to take over the family business, and too sketchy to be sent to the priesthood.

These were the "holy warriors" coming in waves over a total of seven Crusades, up until the thirteenth century, to "liberate" the Holy Land. And frequently, their path included smaller "holy target practices" on any Jews who happened to be in their way.

---

4   In case you're wondering, "How does one even find a guy whose main thing is 'being a hermit,'" welcome to the wonders of faith, my child.

The Crusaders who actually made it to Jerusalem faced reinvigorated Muslim opposition. Between generations of Christian and Arab leaders, Jerusalem changed hands so many times; at one point, both sides agreed to stop fighting and just decide who won the city by "flipping a Cohen."

That's because, despite the Roman expulsion, small communities of Jews continued to live in Judea and Jerusalem throughout the centuries. Their continued presence in Jerusalem was so strong that—while the bigger refugee community in Babylon came up with the entire, voluminous work known as the "Babylonian Talmud"—the scholars of Jerusalem came up with their own "Jerusalem Talmud." Our fights over books go *deep*, people.

NO YORK, NO YORK

Meanwhile, in England, the death of King Henry II in 1189 and the rise of his son Richard I (the Lionheart) set off a fresh wave of "Crusades fever." Not to be confused with the many other kinds of actual medical fever constantly being set off in those times. No, this was a rise in Islamophobic and, yes, anti-Semitic furor.

And soon this rage turned against Jewish moneylenders— one of the few jobs permitted to them. One of these, Benedict of York, was so critical a financier, King Richard invited him to his coronation. But anti-Semites sparked a riot in order to prevent Benedict's entry, wounding him in the process. Then a leading non-Jewish nobleman in York stirred up another mob to attack Jews they owed money to, in order to erase their debts. Hey guys, ever heard of a "financing plan?"

Meanwhile, as rumors spread that King Richard had ordered the Jews expelled from England, anti-Jewish riots erupted, and the Jews of York fled for refuge inside Clifford's Tower. Unfortunately, the sheriff could not hold back the rioters, and the Jews inside chose to take their own lives rather than be killed or forcibly converted. In London, Jews were also being massacred by similar-minded mobs. It was probably little consolation to Jews that they were now part of a hot new nationwide trend.

And anti-Jewish sentiment continued to grow in England. In the thirteenth century, King Edward I completely banned moneylending under the "Statute of Jewry," which is so specifically named as to almost be flattering. Edward hung three hundred Jews, arrested more, and seized their property, all "in the name of the Crown!" Although after a while he got tired of mentioning the whole Crown thing and just went straight to the more fun hanging/arresting/seizing part.

But Edward completed the sentiment in 1290 by issuing the "Edict of Expulsion," which officially banished the Jews from England.

It didn't help that his last words were, "Frightfully sorry, my old Mosaic chums."

UNFAIR

SPAIN BRINGS THE PAIN

From the ninth through the fourteenth century, Muslim Arabs conquered the Iberian Peninsula from the Spanish and Portuguese. Muslim-controlled Spain enjoyed a remarkable period of tolerance, respect, and scholarly interchange between Jews, Christians, and Muslims—and equally remarkably, between Jews and Jews. This period was known as the *Convivencia*, which is Spanish for either "coexistence" or "Are you nerds *still* talking?"

But from 1200 to 1492, militant Christian forces gradually began to retake the area from the Arabs in what they called the *Reconquista* (Spanish for "Uh-oh, Dad's home!"). The Reconquistadors demanded that all residents of Spain be Catholic...or cease being residents of Spain. Authorized by the Vatican, the so-called "Spanish Inquisition"—kind of like the Census but with extremely sharp weapons—jailed, interrogated, tortured, and executed thousands.

And after six hundred years of peace, it was pretty awkward breaking the news to the Jews, based on this completely historically authentic text message chain from the period:

⁓

TORQUEMAN: Yo.

SPANJEWS: Sorry, don't have you in my contacts. Who's this?

TORQUEMAN: Tomás de Torquemada, Grand Inquisitor of Spain!

SPANJEWS: Sorry, "Inquisitor?" What is that?

TORQUEMAN: Oh, just a guy who…asks a lot of questions.

SPANJEWS: U like asking questions just like we do! Nice.

TORQUEMAN: …

SPANJEWS: Connection issues?

TORQUEMAN: …

SPANJEWS: What's going on, Question Guy?

TORQUEMAN: So, funny story. We Catholics just reconquered the land, and now everyone…has to be Catholic.

SPANJEWS: 😨

TORQUEMAN: Just being real with you, my guy.

SPANJEWS: And what if we stay…non-Catholic?

TORQUEMAN: Good news: lotta options for you

SPANJEWS: 👍

TORQEMAN: There's whipping, waterboarding, breaking your body on the rack...

SPANJEWS: WTF?

TORQUEMAN: Also, we're doing this super publicly, in a ceremony we call an "auto-da-fé," where we'll humiliate and possibly torture you into apologizing for being Jewish (or Muslim! We're proud to think of ourselves as heresy-blind).

SPANJEWS: Just kill me bro.

TORQUEMAN: 👍

SPANJEWS: Wait, srsly?

TORQUEMAN: JK. But also, yes.

SPANJEWS: I want to speak to your supervisor.

TORQUEMAN: You mean Spain's King Ferdinand and Queen Isabella? They're totally into this. Sorry. ✌️

SPANJEWS: Supervisor.

TORQUEMAN: Pope Sixtus is unavailable. Also, infallible.

SPANJEWS: Hold up. What if we...pretended to be Catholic? Just keep doing Jewish stuff in secret, but call ourselves something cool and low-key like "conversos?"

TORQUEMAN: Up 2 u but if we catch you, you're 💀 🥩

SPANJEWS: So that's just it, then? 100s of 1000s of Jews, publicly tortured, and forced to abandon their faith?

TORQUEMAN: Don't forget Muslims! ✌️

SPANJEWS: This is definitely the worst breakup text ever.

TORQUEMAN: BRB

TORQUEMAN: So, update: Now we're actually kinda…evicting you. From the entire country.

SPANJEW: *Evicting*? 😲 On what grounds?

TORQUEMAN: You don't eat ham, our national food. You *never* make it to church. You rejected our Lord and Savior. And He's like super-fragile.

SPANJEW: Where are we supposed to go?

TORQUEMAN: IDK. But we'll be sure to give you a terrible reference.

SPANJEW: JFC!

TORQUEMAN: That's not helping.

SPANJEW. So…when do we have to be out of here by?

TORQUEMAN: Will circle back. But rn we're just looking for a year that rhymes with "Columbus sailed the ocean blue."

SETTLING FOR PALE

On the flip side, some Jews weren't *allowed* to leave their country. Millions of Jews lived in Eastern Europe, the Baltic nations, and the Slavic-but-not-necessarily-Russian pieces of Belarus and Ukraine. But those territories were constantly being fought over, claimed in one country's name, then reconquered and claimed in another's. This was, of course, true with most of Europe throughout most of European history. But this particular area was so chronically hard to pin down, even your history teacher is like, "Don't bother learning the map! Just write down whatever you remember while I slip outside for my morning Jack-Daniels-hidden-in-my-coffee-cup cry."

Then, in 1762, Catherine the Great became tsarina of Russia, conquered large swathes of Poland and Turkey in war—and wanted to make sure Poland and Turkey never took them back. And she thought, "Which population is used to being herded around, has no rights, and would be really skillful at absorbing cannonballs from our enemies to the East?"

Ding ding ding! That's right, the Jews! And so Catherine, and the next Tsar, Paul, decreed that Jews now had to *stay* in those freshly conquered territories as a human buffer zone. They termed this area the "Pale of Settlement"—presumably after taking one glance at the residents' skin tone.

THE ROTHSCHILDS

As mentioned, since European Jews were banned from so many occupations, many found a new way to make a living: banking. Christianity forbade the lending of money with interest, and this had been a significant obstacle to the expansion of businesses. But the rule did not apply to non-Christians, so Jews came in to fill that need. For the first and perhaps only point in their history, the Jews finally had good timing!

And as Europe entered an age of exploration, its governments found themselves in greater need of capital. This led to the rise of massively successful Jewish-run banks to help fund their endeavors. Or specifically, families like the Rothschilds.

Mayer Rothschild was born in 1744 in Frankfurt, Germany, the bustling commercial heart of the Holy Roman Empire—where Jews had to live in an enforced ghetto and were restricted to only twelve weddings a year. This was unbelievably tough on Jews, although a welcome reprieve to drinking glasses.

When Mayer was twelve, his parents died of smallpox, leaving him to take care of four younger siblings. Poor guy. But not poor for long! Rothschild went on to work for a crown prince who dealt in rare coins, medals, and Hessians (German mercenaries available for rent to any country at war). And in late eighteenth century Europe, war was a "growth industry." Which meant more profit for Mayer and his boss.

That's right. At one point in history, a Jewish father came home and told his family, "Great news, guys! War in Europe and German soldiers on the rise!"

And soon Mayer's dealings took him abroad to other foreign capitals, where he made contacts he would later use to build an international business empire. As the French Revolution and Napoleon and other forces kept Europe embroiled in war, the need for cash kept mounting. Rothschild and his children became the ATM of Europe, and the lines went around the block.

Their children's children continued the family business, and soon the Rothschilds, along with a few other Jewish families, had become a banking powerhouse that continues to this day.

Your move, smallpox.

Now, right about now, if you're seeing the phrase "small wealthy group of Jews financing world affairs" and wondering if you've stumbled onto a Bad Part of the internet (or honestly, just the internet), you're not alone. This image of a Jewish cabal behind the scenes, bankrolling giant and tumultuous historic events, caught on like wildfire—most of which Jews were blamed for too.

And it gets worse. An entire notion took off that a "small group" (who are not necessarily but, let's face it, probably believed to be Jews) engineered and profited from global catastrophes. It was an idea that would be consistently applied to every world-shaking event, from the Napoleonic Wars to both World Wars, even right down to present day (see p. 209). So every time you hear something blamed on international Jewish donor-activist George Soros, make sure to tell the blamer, "Congratulations on having the good sense of an eighteenth century European!"

The twin genius of this concept was:

a) It explained *everything* at a time when the Scientific Revolution claimed to be explaining everything but was really barely getting the job done.

b) Jew-blame was *so convenient* because most angry people happened to have a Jew or two on hand to take said anger out on.[5]

POGROMS: IT TAKES A VILLAGE

And that collective Jew-focused anger still festered, even after Europe had entered the supposed Age of Enlightenment. Not that that age was particularly enlightened towards women or men who were not themselves dermatologically "lightened." But as always, the consistent hallmark of a global movement for higher ideals and better treatment of people is "except Jews."

In this case, remember that fun "pre-urban legend" that the Jews had killed Jesus and were now killing contemporary Christian children? The propagation of this belief riled up European peasants—sometimes abetted by leaders and officials—to launch pogroms, or waves of bloody annihilation against entire Jewish villages. That's right, vengeance brigades sponsored by the religion that brought you "turn the other cheek."

Jews have endured pogroms for centuries, from the Middle Ages to the era of instability between the world wars; to the infamous 1938 Nazi-organized assault on German Jewish businesses known as Kristallnacht; to ones against Jewish communities in Iraq, Libya, Syria, and Turkey in the years after the founding of the state of Israel; and the October 7, 2023, massacre in Israel by Hamas.

But a particularly large wave of them struck Eastern European Jews in the late nineteenth century. Sizable ones

---

5   This is probably the reason why Jews came up with the concept of "therapy."

took place in Odessa, Warsaw, and Bialystok. A particularly notorious one in Kishinev in 1903 inspired a brutal poem called "In the City of Slaughter," by the poet Hayim Nahman Bialik, great-great-great-granduncle of American sitcom superstar Mayim Bialik. Suffice it to say this was the furthest thing imaginable from a laugh track.

The Kishinev pogrom also marked a kind of tipping point for the then-burgeoning Zionist movement. Their argument: "Clearly, Jews will be attacked wherever we live in Europe. Why don't we just settle down in a more peaceful, Jew-welcoming place...

"...like the Middle East?"

THE INFLUENCER INTERVIEW

ANNIE: Hey guys, it's your girl Annie Freshlife here, and today I am so stoked to be talking to Isaac Luria, a totally real dead rabbi joining us from the Holy Land!

ISAAC: Thank you, Annie.

ANNIE: First of all, can I just say, for a guy born in 1572, you look *ah-mazing*. Is it because you lived up on a mountaintop in the city of Tzfat, Israel? I loooove mountaintops. The *best* backgrounds for selfies! Hashtag no filter!

ISAAC: ...okay?

ANNIE: Anyway, I brought you on to talk about Kabbalah, which is like this crazy ancient Jewish wisdom about energy and meditation, according to a guy I do cleanses with. What is it, Rabbi L?

ISAAC: Well, Kabbalah is the mystical tradition of Jewish learning and contemplation, which believes that God is a force, made up of many specific kinds of attributes, called *sefirot*.

ANNIE: Whooaa...

ISAAC: I know, it's a lot to take in.

ANNIE: No, I was just checking my views since you started talking. Blowing up!

ISAAC: What?! Are we going to die?

ANNIE: No, it means…eh, it's too complicated to explain. Let's get back to something simpler: Kabbalah.

ISAAC: OK.

ANNIE: So you said God is made of…"attributes," was it? What are we talking, like, "great dancer?" "Perfect eyebrows?" "Raises money for dolphin rescue?"

ISAAC: Not exactly. More, um, enduring traits like wisdom, understanding, mercy, justice, beauty, eternity, glory, and foundation.

ANNIE: Speaking of foundation, remind me to tell you guys about Hello Beautiful Skin Elixir, a new product that has *literally* transformed my morning regimen!

ISAAC: Right… So, anyway, Kabbalah says that the Torah is not only a chronicle of history and laws. It also tells the unfolding story of those divine attributes entering our world and acting in it, often in mystical ways outside of the main narrative.

ANNIE: So, like, fan fiction?

ISAAC: No, that's a different body of rabbinic literature called Midrash. Kabbalah is more of an action guide for how we humans can help God manifest those attributes.

ANNIE: Did you know I *just* manifested that a laser teeth-whitening appointment with Harmony would open up, and then it *totally did!*

ISAAC: I cannot say that I knew that, no.

ANNIE: So where did, like, all this Kabbalah stuff *come* from?

ISAAC: We believe Shimon bar Yochai, a second century CE rabbi, first learned Kabbalah from the Prophet Elijah and wrote it down in a book we study called the Zohar. And a group of us led by my rabbi, Moses Cordovero, and populated by some folks who fled here from Spain after the Inquisition, started a school to study it here in Tzfat.

ANNIE: Wait a minute... Don't scholars believe that the Zohar was more likely actually written by Moses de León in the thirteenth century?

ISAAC: Impressive! Someone did her homework.

ANNIE: Being prepared is the ultimate lifestyle hack! But I didn't mean the actual history. I mean, like, how did the divine attributes get here—into our world—in the first place?

ISAAC: Well, Kabbalah teaches that at the time of Creation, our plane of existence was too limited to contain all of God's grandeur. And so the world actually shattered, spilling little sparks of that divinity everywhere. But through performing mitzvot—Jewish commandments—and refining our spiritual nature, we have the power to redeem all those shattered sparks.

ANNIE: Whoa...

ISAAC: What? Are we losing viewers???

ANNIE: No, I'm just…wow. So you're saying that someone like me, lighting a Shabbat candle, saying morning prayers, even avoiding bacon, can actually help *repair the world?*

ISAAC: Buh-buh-buh, don't badmouth bacon! People like bacon. We're losing them, Annie!

ANNIE: Well, then, tell the viewers where we can find Kabbalah! Do you guys have, like, an events calendar?

ISAAC: In just about any synagogue every Friday night! The Kabbalat Shabbat service was invented by us. Two of my Kabbalah-studying colleagues wrote the famous songs "Lecha Dodi" and "Yedid Nefesh" that are still sung every week.

ANNIE: You guys have been charting for five hundred years???

ISAAC: Not only that, but our concept that all humans have a specific, concrete role in "repairing" the world's shattered sparks, or *tikkun olam,* has inspired countless Jews to devote their lives to fixing the world in other ways. And our turn towards spiritualism was also a huge factor behind the rise of *Hasidut.*

ANNIE: What's "*Hasidut?*"

ISAAC: We'll get to that next. But first, it's time for your ad read for Hello Beautiful Skin Elixir.

THE THREE GREAT JEWISH CHILLOUTS

By the end of the Middle Ages, being Jewish had gotten… intense. When Jews weren't getting discriminated against, pillaged, or worse, they were getting expelled. At the same time, Johannes Gutenberg (who wasn't Jewish even though his name sounds like it) invented the printing press. This led to an explosion of books, and specifically major rabbinic commentaries—making Jewish text study more serious than ever.

It seemed like being a Jew meant you were always on the run or on the read. But what if there was…another way?

HASIDUT - THE JEWS GET SOUL

In the eighteenth century, in what was then Poland but is now Ukraine, lived a rabbi named Israel ben Eliezer (also known as the "Baal Shem Tov," or "Master of the Good Name" or the "Besht," or less popularly, "Nicknames McGee"). He followed the classic path well-trodden by countless brilliant young men in the Jewish tradition: getting bored in Hebrew school.

Well, technically he was a teacher not a student, and it wasn't "bored" so much as "spiritually dead," but the point is, the Baal Shem Tov rebelled. And not in the ways that most Hebrew school burnouts do: throwing spitballs, hiding secret scandalous works in the prayer book, slowly drifting away from Judaism into Scientology.

No, Baal Shem Tov was way too Type-Aleph for that. He reinvented Judaism as a religion of spirituality. He urged his students to try and find God in the text as well as in their hearts. He took them outside of the airless study hall into the woods to experience connection with the divine. He also poured them a *lot* of vodka.

Soon the Besht had attracted many followers throughout Poland, Lithuania, the Pale, and far beyond to his fresh joy-filled, vodka-scented approach. They called this movement *Hasidut* ("pietism") and themselves Hasidic.

But as happens with any major revolution, a counterrevolution followed. *Hasidut* soon found itself with opponents calling themselves Mitnagdim, or "opponents." Admittedly, this is a less creative title, but still—it's nice that they didn't have to do anything but still got their own nickname.

The Mitnagdim rankled at *Hasidut*'s deemphasizing of the Talmud as the end-all be-all of study. They got irritated at these hippy-dippy types obsessing—sometimes literally for hours!—over things like the "spiritual intentions" before, say, blowing a shofar.

Mostly, they hate-hate-*hated* that this self-proclaimed magical mystic Baal Shem Tov was a threat to their authority! If these guys could break off and "Jew their own thing" with their own rebbe, what was to stop others? And indeed, the Mitnagdim were right (as they would probably be the first to remind you). Many Hasidic sects did break off, many of which (for example: Satmar, Breslov, and Chabad) are still around and known by their founders' name today.

It's hard to appreciate just how revolutionary the term "Hasidism" once was. Nowadays, when many people hear "Hasidic Jew," they think "member of a rigidly observant patriarchal army that dresses like they're still in eighteenth century Eastern Europe." But the Hasidim were the wild-eyed Burning-Man attendees of their time, only less tan and with schnapps instead of LSD.

HASKALAH – THE JEWS GET SCHOOLED

If, for some incomprehensible reason, you've ever read a book of *non*-Jewish history, you may recall that in Europe, the Middle Ages gave way to the Renaissance, Enlightenment, and the Scientific Revolution. People stopped being satisfied with the explanation "Because an old white guy in the sky said so" and started demanding to hear "Because a bunch of old white guys in Vienna said so."

Well, similar waves of skepticism and curiosity were on the rise within Judaism. Centering around Berlin in the late 1700s, a group of scholars began to study the Hebrew language and Jewish texts more like scientists. That is, as a systematic body of knowledge—not as grad students weeping into a pile of unfinished grant applications.

This modern approach to ancient scriptures unearthed uncomfortable questions: *What if God didn't write all this? What if humans did? What if some of the humans who did write it were dicks?*

And if God's authorship was in question, what did this suggest about God's authority? Hasidic troublemakers aside, the Rabbis had claimed to have an unbroken chain of leadership going back to Moses. These new claims of scientific knowledge directly threatened all of that.

Proponents of this new approach to Judaism called themselves Maskilim, or the "enlightened ones," which makes them sound more like a weird white-robed sunglass cult than the stuffy Germanic scholars in dark three-piece suits they were.

One of their leaders was Moses Mendelssohn, a scholar who translated the Torah into the more accessible German and tried to meld traditional Jewish values with the (then) cutting-edge ideas of modernity. Mendelssohn described his ideal of modern Jews as "men on the street and Jews at home." No word on what he thought they should be in the sheets.

Furthermore, in their schools, Jewish students were still often learning only Jewish topics. The Maskilim wanted them to also start learning science, math, literature, and most terrifyingly, PE. They started their own Jewish day schools reflecting this new balance of subjects. Unfortunately, to students, some of these schools seemed to be influenced by that other recently developed Germanic discipline, sadomasochism.

And while expanding Jewish scholarship into the ever-widening fields of worldly study, the Maskilim also brought more worldliness into Judaism. Movements sprang up that considered Judaism more of an "option" than an all-encompassing way of life. Orthodox, Reform, Conservative, and Reconstructionist denominations became the norm (see p. 133), each choosing their own balance between Jewish ritual observance and belonging to a wider Christian state. And most important of all, their own distinctive headwear.

Meanwhile, tensions grew between the traditional life of the shtetl, and the appealing new opportunities offered by…

URBANIZATION – THE JEWS GET GOING

For centuries, most European Jews tended to live in the same tiny, stinky, and all-too-flammable villages, often known as shtetls or ghettos. This was due to many factors: traditional Jewish insularity, the relentless labor demands of an agricultural economy, and Christian authorities declaring, "Yeah no, you have to just stay on this dirt patch forever, especially after what you did to our Lord."

That changed, however, when Napoleon took over France in the late 1800s. Among his other sweeping changes, Napoleon told the Jews they were free to leave the ghettos for the newly tolerant cities and enjoy equality with their fellow citizens. This was called "emancipation," or as some Jews called it, "thank God I never have to clean up another goat turd."

Other European cities followed the lead of the so-called "Napoleonic Laws" and put up banners saying "Welcome Jews!" or at least, "We'll Try Really Hard Not to Burn Your House Down and Steal Your Stuff, Jews!"

And while many Jews did remain behind, many others left the shtetls and ghettos and sought their fortune in the wide range of new professions and fields now being opened to them across Europe.

Unfortunately, with the newly popular eighteenth to nineteenth century European idea of "nationhood," the Original Sin of Jews shifted from "You killed Jesus" to "you're not a *real* German." But this was just another sign of the delightful exuberance of anti-Semitism—seemingly able to reinvent itself as often as the Jews did. In fact, it was even a German, Wilhelm Marr, who invented the term "Antisemitismus" in 1867. They really *do* have a word for everything!

However, once the borders of their shtetls had been breached, the whole world was these Jews' oyster. And with many of them abandoning not just their traditional homes but also Jewish law, so were…oysters.

PART 3

SAMUEL PALLACHE
MERCHANT/DIPLOMAT/PIRATE
MOROCCO, 15TH CENTURY CE

That's right, you read that correctly: *Jewish Pirate*. According to legend, there were quite a few of us. And it just makes sense! After the Spanish Inquisition, many of us fled to the New World, where we became swashbuckling merchant adventurers preying on the Spanish treasure fleet. Some of us wanted to take revenge on ships bearing the flag of Spain. Some of us needed new employment after the Inquisition suddenly gave us an unplanned "career pivot." And some of us just wanted the *gelt*. Now you might not necessarily associate "searching the globe for buried treasure" with the Jews. But then again, we did spend forty years wandering the desert on a trip that should have taken eleven days.

Other Spanish exiles fled across the Strait of Gibraltar to nearby Morocco. Jews had actually lived in Morocco since the destruction of the first Temple...and boy did they never tire of telling you about it! But soon, this new influx of migrants with skills in translation and commerce came to occupy prominent positions in society and the royal court—even though most were just given the catchall title of "Court Jew."

As for me, I became the Sultan of Morocco's commercial and diplomatic agent in Holland. Then I switched it up, working as an informer revealing Moroccan secrets to authorities in Spain. I split my time between Morocco, Spain, and the Netherlands—and depending on which country I was in, I would shift back and forth between Jewish and Catholic. It may sound confusing, but I stayed anchored between both faiths through the constancy of guilt and maternal disapproval.

RADAI
DYNASTIC CHIEF
ETHIOPIA, 16TH CENTURY CE

We Ethiopian Jews have a long history, dating back to King Solomon's one-night stand with the Queen of Sheba back in the tenth century BCE. Apparently, he wasn't wise enough to use birth control. On the other hand, what else would you expect from a guy who had seven hundred wives and three hundred concubines?

The product of this union was our legendary founder Menelik (which translates to "The One Who Keeps Getting Uncomfortable Questions About His Paternity.") Some even say that Menelik once came to visit Solomon in Jerusalem and left in possession of the Ark of the Covenant. There's nothing a "weekend Dad" won't do to get his kids to like him.

Others say we're not descended from Menelik, but rather from the lost tribe of Dan, separated from the other eleven during the Northern/Southern civil war. Still other say we were brought to Ethiopia as prisoners of war. There are many theories about how Jews got to Ethiopia, but it's important to focus on the main point: We got there and found somebody to despise us.

Actually, despite occasional tribal warfare, we Ethiopian Jews mostly lived separately from non-Jews and Jews alike. We had our own spin on Jewish traditions and texts. We don't follow the Talmud and rabbinic law, which makes things *so* much simpler when, say, executing a child for insulting their parents.[1]

We do follow the Jewish lunar calendar but also have our own holidays and our own language (called "Ge'ez") that our Jewish scriptures are written in. And speaking of those, in place of your Pentateuch (the five books of Moses), we have an Octateuch that also includes Joshua, Judges, and Ruth. Which makes our Torah like *three times better* than yours.

We're also the only Jewish community with monks—an extraordinary accomplishment when you remember how hard it is for a Jew to stay silent. And in my time, we even established our own mini kingdom called Beta Israel inside the host country of Ethiopia.

When King Sarsa Dengel tried to conquer it, my rebels and I thwarted the king's troops using an advanced military tactic called "climbing into the mountains and dropping rocks on them." Don't press me too hard on the details because there's just no simple way to explain it.

ZHANG MEI
CLAN LEADER
KAIFENG, CHINA, 17TH CENTURY CE

"Jews in…China?! What did they eat on Christmas Eve?" I've heard all the jokes. But yes, we made it all the way to the Far East, most likely descended from Persian and Bukharan merchants.

---

1   Deuteronomy 21:18–21 (JPS 2023), and Talmud, Sanhedrin Chapter 8 (*The William Davidson Talmud, Sanhedrin 68b, Sefaria, accessed September 10, 2024, https://www.sefaria.org/Sanhedrin.68b).* Go look it up and then quickly apologize to your parents!

There were many signs left behind documenting our time in China, including two ancient columns inscribed with details of Jewish genealogy and practice. These became much easier to record once we'd discovered easier surfaces to write on than *columns*. And the first proofs of Jewish settlement in China date back to around the tenth century CE Song Dynasty. We wrote down our family names in a giant tome called the Memory Book. Embarrassingly enough, I can't recall where I left it.

Over the centuries, we tried really hard to integrate into our host culture: intermarrying, giving ourselves Chinese names, and even adopting the local custom of foot-binding (which explains why there are so many Jewish podiatrists).

Some of us tried so hard to meld with the locals, we even practiced polygamous marriages. In fact, I myself had six wives! That's right—as many as Jacob and Abraham combined. Who's your patriarch *now*?

GLUCKEL OF HAMELN
BUSINESSWOMAN/DIARIST
HAMBURG, GERMANY, 18TH CENTURY CE

In my time, Jews in Europe still weren't admitted into most high-level professions. So many who lived in port cities, like my husband and I, engaged in trade. Hayyim and I traveled all around Europe slinging more pearls than a belligerent oyster. I helped run the business and took it over after he died, all while raising thirteen children. My only regret is not having a high school reunion to go back and rub this in everyone's face at.

After the death of my dear Hayyim, I decided to try writing as well. I penned my famous diary, which is the only early modern Yiddish memoir written by a woman. And as an added bonus, the only one written by me!

My diaries describe what life was like for Northern German Jews during a period of history that includes the Khmelnytsky Uprising (which left thousands of Jews dead), the false Jewish messiah Sabbatai Zevi, and the War of the Spanish Succession.

I also covered rugby and local weather.

OY! GAYS!

It would be tricky to reduce an account of LGBTQ+ people throughout Jewish history to one word. But that word would definitely not be *invisible*.

Admittedly, male homosexuality and Judaism do not get off to a good start. Leviticus 18:22 says, "Do not lie with a male as one lies with a woman; it is an abhorrence" (JPS 1985), with the "you" implied to be a male reader or listener. Genesis's account of the city of Sodom, so sinful it had to be destroyed by God, is the origin of the word "sodomy." Which is frankly absurd, since from the story, the clear sin of the Sodomites is being horrible to tourists.

But later on, in the first book of Samuel, the story of **David** (see p. 51) includes a significant subplot about his relationship with King Saul's son **Jonathan.** Let's just say it was a *close* relationship. Jonathan is described as someone whose "soul became bound up with David" (1 Sam 18:1, JPS 1985). He dresses David (1 Sam 18:4, JPS 1985). They kiss (1 Sam 20:41, JPS 195). David characterizes Jonathan's love as more wonderful "than the love of women" (2 Sam 1:26, JPS 1985) Just about the only thing missing is Jonathan running to the airport to stop David from getting on that plane.

Intriguingly, the Torah is completely silent about lesbianism. An early Midrash on Leviticus called Sifra bans it, but only because it's said to resemble an idolatrous practice by the Egyptians. The main concern of the Talmudic rabbis is whether a prior lesbian relationship disqualifies a woman from marrying a priest since priests are only allowed to marry virgins. The twelfth century commentator **Maimonides** (see p. 94) stringently warns men to keep their wives away from lesbians. Feeling a little threatened there, Rambam?

As for the Levitical prohibition on male homosexuality, the Talmud takes it literally and, as in most traditional cultures, outright bans being out. Still, the Talmud is a wide-ranging, topically sprawling, and just plain *huge* work, and it takes a few surprising turns on this spicy subject.

For one thing, it describes, in clinical detail, as many as eight different types of "genders" people can be born with. This is not to say the rabbinic position was "Gender is a construct—*free your mind!*" But it's intriguing that these ancient sages recognized the complexity of human genders at a time when they also believed you could cure a fever by sealing an ant up in a copper tube.[1]

There's also a highly *suggestive* story about the great rabbis **Yohanan** and **Reish Lakish** essentially frolicking in a river naked with a lance. As with David and Jonathan, the tale can be interpreted many ways—but this reading is unquestionably the hottest.

In later centuries, some wandering Jews let their thoughts wander over the rainbow. From 900–1200 CE, Spanish Jewish poets like **Moses Ibn Ezra** and **Yehuda Halevi** (see p. 93) penned works full of language that can easily be read as homoerotic. This is significant because they were not outlier figures in the tradition. Both also wrote liturgy that is still

---

1   Yes, it's real—look it up. (*The William Davidson Talmud*, Shabbat 66b:22, Sefaria, accessed September 10, 2024, https://www.sefaria.org/Shabbat.66b.23)

used in Shabbat and festival prayerbooks. There was no contradiction between "gay" and "pray."

More homoerotic imagery came from **Kalonymus ben Kalonymus**, a thirteenth century German poet and, apparently, a nepo baby. And a responsum (legal opinion) from the sixteenth century tells a very lurid tale of **Moshko** and his many public dalliances with "bachelors." Except that he gave these bachelors something a bit more intimate than a rose.

Leaping ahead to modern times, acceptance began to slowly emerge. In 1907, playwright **Sholem Asch** penned a play for the Yiddish theater called *Got fun Nekome* (*God of Vengeance*), which featured a lesbian subplot and several homoerotic scenes. It was a smash hit, playing in Europe and America, and eventually moving to Broadway in English. Unfortunately, a citizen-run "anti-vice" group had the actors arrested and tried to shut down the play. Which, sadly, is still a better run than most Broadway plays get.

The various Jewish denominations emerging in the nineteenth and twentieth centuries (see p. 133) confronted the question of homosexuality in Judaism in differing ways. Big surprise there, I know.

The most liberal denomination, the Reform movement, recognized the first-ever LGBTQIA+ synagogue, **Beth Chayim Chadashim**, in 1972. In 1978, they ordained the first openly gay rabbi, **Allen Bennett**. Reconstructionism opened the doors even wider in the 1980s. In 2006, the Conservative movement issued an opinion on the matter that was highly technical, unworkable, and didn't quite satisfy anyone—which is pretty much their stock in trade.

Nowadays, there are many LGBTQIA+ synagogues, like New York's **Congregation Beit Simchat Torah**, which was a critical community during the AIDS crisis and continues to be a home for LGBTQIA+ Jews today. Same-sex marriages have become normalized in Reform, Reconstructionism, and most of Conservatism. Traditions are being reconsidered, and ancient heteronormative language is being retranslated and reinterpreted. **Rabbi Elliot Kukla** is the first openly transgender person to be ordained as Rabbi and is helping expand Jewish rituals to be even more inclusive. A large percentage of Jews seem fine with this—as long as he doesn't make services last any longer.

And while the more traditional Hasidic, Haredi, and Chabad Orthodox groups are firm in their rejection of homosexuality, there are some flickers of tolerance in the mainstream and Modern Orthodox branches. Organizations like **Eshel** help parents of Orthodox LGBTQIA+ youth find their place in the community. In other words, homosexuality has reached the critical pinnacle of acceptance in our religion: being argued about a lot by Jews.

Finally outside of religion, LGBTQIA+ Jews have made their mark far and wide.

Violinist **Vladimir Horowitz**, singer **Lesley Gore**, and record mogul **David Geffen** have been huge in twentieth century music. **Marcel Proust, Susan Sontag, Maurice Sendak**, and **Eve Ensler's** literary influence is still formidable. Mayor **Harvey Milk**, Congressman **Barney Frank**, and the first openly gay US Governor **Jared Polis** have been trailblazers in politics. **Joey Soloway** and **Ilene Chaiken** have created groundbreaking television. And **Leonard Bernstein** and **Stephen Sondheim** and their progeny have left such a mark on Broadway, they may have to rename The Great White Way…well, whatever race it is that Jews *actually are*.

But that's a whole other book.

IF NOT NOW, WHEN?

NEW WAYS TO JEW

In the modern era, Judaism faced an existential crisis. Not to be confused, of course, with the existential crises that faced pre-modern, Renaissance, Medieval, Exilic, and Biblical Judaism.

Once liberated from the shtetls and ghettoes and set loose in the big city, Jews suddenly found themselves with…choices. Not something they'd had a lot of before. Choices on how to be Jewish. When to be Jewish. Where. If.

For many, the modern world with its glittering enticements was irresistible, but so was the pull of their tradition. They wanted a way to honor both. Fortunately, we've managed to bring together four top minds from this era to make their pitch for "the future of Jew!"

First up, Rabbi Abraham Geiger from nineteenth-century Germany.

GEIGER: Thank you, Invisible Book Guy. As you said, we're facing a crisis! Jews are abandoning the shtetls in big numbers for the big cities…but they're also abandoning Judaism. The good news is, we have a solution. Unlike our ancestors, we live in a world of unprecedented scientific advances and individual liberties. So we need a new kind of Judaism to reflect that. Today's scholars have shown that the Torah wasn't received directly from Sinai—which means we are not under divine obligation to obey its many cumbersome laws. So we say: follow the science, lighten the legal load, and more Jews will want to stay Jewish! I call it "Reform Judaism," but hey man, call it whatever you're feeling!

Thanks, Rabbi Geiger. Now I would guess that your nineteenth-century German counterpart, Rabbi Samson Raphael Hirsch, completely disagrees.

HIRSCH: I do, indeed. Do you not see what an *unprecedented opportunity* we've been handed? For the first time since living in the land of Israel, our host nations are saying "Go ahead, practice your religion however you want." We can use contemporary scholarship to better understand our traditional texts. We can work in the modern world and inspire the goyim with Jewish values. We can finally be true to our traditions without fear. It's a smorgasbord—and we are a people whose motto is "Eat, eat!"

So…just keep observing all the Torah and halacha like before?

HIRSCH: Yes, but now we'll rebrand it as "Orthodox Judaism." Or as we used to call it, "Judaism."

Alright, over in the twentieth century in America, we've got Rabbi Mordecai Kaplan. Now Rabbi, I saw you frowning during the other rabbis' pitches. How would you "sell Jew" differently?

KAPLAN: Thanks, IBG. The problem with Reform and Orthodoxy is that they both present the observance of laws and rituals as a binary choice: "Take it or leave it." Neither answers the question, "What do we think of the rituals themselves?" So to keep modern Jews interested, I say we need to reinvent or *reconstruct* entirely new ways to be Jewish. I'd call it "Reconstructionism"—a name I totally just invented, on the spot, to perfectly meet the needs of this moment. See how easy this is?

HIRSCH: Oh *great* idea! Why don't we just "reinvent" Judaism as a religion where we ride on giant three-toed sloths and drink rotten milk every third Tuesday?

Excuse me, Rabbi Hirsch, I'm the one asking the questions here? And I'd...also like to know about the sloth/rotten milk/ Tuesday thing.

KAPLAN: Look, all religion is ultimately made up at some point! Does it make *sense* that we wave a bunch of branches around in a hut every autumn or cleanse our soul of sins by starving for twenty-five hours?

OK, Rabbi Solomon Schechter, you're also joining us from twentieth-century America. What is your pitch for enabling Jews to straddle both the modern world and traditional Judaism?

SCHECHTER: Um...what if we just did something like... in the middle?

I'm sorry, could you elaborate?

SCHECHTER: Some of you want to eliminate observance, others to keep it, others to change it. What if we just did... some of all of that? I'd call it "Conservative Judaism," which is a name that doesn't startle anyone and embosses nicely on leatherbound objects.

GEIGER: I agree. Every Jew in every generation should be free to do some. Or…none?

HIRSCH: Then they'll all choose "none!" Because in essence you're telling them, "Just do the easy stuff. Fry a potato at Chanukah. Dip an apple in honey at Rosh Hashanah. Nosh on some matzo at Pes–" I really should have eaten before this, shouldn't I.

KAPLAN: But Samson, some of the "other stuff" you Orthodox are clinging to isn't relevant to them any more in this rapidly changing, way more complicated world. What if people really *do* draw enormous personal meaning from a three-toed sloth?

SCHECHTER: Guys, can we compromise? What if it was just a one-toed sloth…or a one-and-a-half-toed sloth?

OK, that's all the time we have! Thank you to the founders of Reform, Orthodox, Reconstructionist, and Conservative Judaism. May the best movement win! Or—to manage expectations within Jewish history—survive.

HOMELAND WANTED

At the end of the nineteenth century, Jews in many parts of Europe were facing a harrowing rise in state-permitted anti-Semitic attacks on their communities. They began to call for a specifically Jewish state of their own (and no, southern Florida didn't count). Representatives from different nations began meeting in a series of what were called "Zionist Congresses," to plot out how a Jewish homeland could be achieved. After dismissing the idea of putting one in Uganda (seriously!), Zionist leaders began posting notices for their desired residence. However, you might say these "future roomies" had slightly different visions of what kind of place they were looking for...

OFFICIAL "NATION-PAD" WANTED
CONTACT: Theodor Herzl, Vienna

Hi, Theo here. I'm an Austrian Jewish journalist who wasn't that connected to my Judaism. Then I took a job in Paris and covered the Dreyfus affair for my hometown paper. Albert Dreyfus was a Jewish French army captain who was falsely accused of spying for Germany and sent to prison after mass anti-Semitic rallies. I saw that and reached the conclusion that Jews are about as safe in France as buttered snails.

And when I looked across turn-of-the-twentieth-century Europe, I noticed the same thing: pogroms and new forms of nationalism-based discrimination. And also that, no matter what they wore, turn-of-the-twentieth-century Europeans continued to look ridiculous at the beach.

So I published a pamphlet called *Der Judenstaat* (*The Jewish State*), which caught fire in this pamphlet-obsessed era. And I convened the First Zionist Congress in 1897. Here's what we were looking for in a country:

- o Recognized borders

- o Secure flyover space including air rights and beach access

- o Political charter from international institutions and the community of nations

- o A country large enough to contain one (1) global Jewish community, yet small enough to allow Hebrew school teachers to unroll a map and make a huge deal over that country's tininess

- o And most of all, a safe haven for all Jewish religious and political expression (except maybe those "Jews for Jesus" clowns, because huh? Pick a lane, brother.)

I'm credited with the inspirational saying, "If you will it, it is no dream." (Though in fairness, I wasn't referring to a Jewish state, but rather trying to squeeze into a set of skimpy European swimwear.)

SEEKING: CULTURAL REVIVAL SPRINGBOARD
CONTACT: Ahad Ha'am, Ukraine

I was born Asher Ginsberg but eventually changed my name to "Ahad Ha'am," which is Hebrew for "one of the people." (Or as I like to think of it, "I'm number one! I'm number one!")

And I do spend a lot of my time thinking about my people. Specifically, the ones who—like me—were raised traditionally but sought out further Western education. To me, in this fast-changing era, when tradition and modernity collide, it's exciting to be Jewish! And no, I don't mean "exciting" in the classic sense it has for Jews, which is mainly running from beefy guys on horseback with swords.

So when I see folks like Herzl and these Zionist Congresses planning out a potential Jewish state in Palestine, I think they're limiting themselves by making it just another generic nation-state. I mean, what are we, Belgium? (If only we could *just be Belgium*!)

No, we should also choose to refashion Israel as a brand-new kind of *cultural* homeland for the Jewish people. I made this point forcefully in my first published essay, "Lo Ze ha-Derekh," Hebrew for "This Is Not the Way." (Which, unfortunately, got a little lost among the 1,564 other "This Is Not the Way" essays I wrote, most of which focused on getting tea stains out of furniture.)

To me, the "Political Zionists" are missing a great opportunity to reinvent what it means for this five thousand-year-old people to become a country again. I mean *besides* entering cheesy songs in European contests someday.

So here's what I and my fellow "Cultural Zionists" are looking for in a place:

- One centrally located landmass, where a revitalized Hebrew language will one day be spoken—including ancient biblical words such as "internet," "discount," and "sorry"

- ○ A massive Jewish cultural center for archiving, creating, and promoting Jewish culture around the world

- ○ And, in keeping with the tone of this modern Israel, terrible parking

I'm most famous for saying Israel should be "a Jewish state, not merely a state of Jews." Because I think we already know what the state of Jews is: *frazzled*.

WANTED: ALL OF THE LAND, NOW
CONTACT: Ze'ev Jabotinsky, Odessa

I grew up in Russia, even more distanced from my Jewish heritage. But boy, did I begin to notice it when the pogroms started up again! That particularly bloody one in 1903 in Kishinev, Moldova, was a wakeup call for a lot of us.

I started going to the Zionist Congresses, but my take on political Zionism was more militant than that vegetarian peacemonger Herzl. I thought the problem was that, in exile, we Jews had gotten soft, flabby, and vulnerable. This was why we kept getting picked on in history's locker room.

By contrast, no one would mess with Jews who were big, muscular, and kicking tuchus. We Jews had to do a full image makeover, or at least start powerlifting something besides volumes of Talmud.

So I devoted my life to this militant strain of Zionism. I organized Jewish self-defense units across Russia. In the first World War, I fought for the British in a unit called the "Zion Mule Corps" (not quite as sexy as the name makes it sound). In 1939, I tried to launch a rebellion against the British in Palestine. In 1940, I offered the British a 130,000-member

Jewish volunteer corps to help them against the Nazis. One of the themes of my life has been "confusing relationship with the British."

But I was never confused about the absolute necessity for the Jews to fight. This is why I founded the militant organization Irgun, which fought the British and Arabs for decades before statehood, pursued more extreme measures than its mainstream rival the Haganah, and carried out the infamous bombing of the King David Hotel (Britain's military headquarters in Jerusalem)—which almost certainly lowered its rating to four stars.

MESSIANIC ERA WANTED, STAT!
CONTACT: Rabbi Abraham Isaac Kook, Jerusalem

I was a nice Jewish boy. Went to yeshiva, became a rabbi at twenty-three. Then I was invited to become the chief rabbi of Yaffo, an ancient town next to today's Tel Aviv. Later, I rose to become Ashkenazi Chief Rabbi of Jerusalem, then eventually Ashkenazi Chief Rabbi of Palestine. My lust for incredibly niche power was insatiable!

But when it came to founding a modern Jewish state, I ruffled more feathers than a kosher butcher preparing for the end of Yom Kippur. Many traditional (or, as they began calling themselves, "Orthodox") authorities opposed Zionism. Not the idea of it, but because of its non-religious nature. They were expecting the return to our homeland to come about through divine, not human means.

By contrast, Uncle Izzy—digging up swamps with his fellow secular-educated, non-kosher-keeping, "Which holiday is

Shavuot again?" veterans from the Zion Mule Corps—did not exactly fulfill this glorious vision.

But I firmly believed that even the "earthly" return to the Land was part of a larger spiritual redemption. One which was led by the secularists because they were willing to get their hands dirty and do the schmoozing with non-Jewish authorities that the job required. Once the ground was cleared and the cities built, we religious folk would march in and pick up right where our predecessors had left off two thousand years ago.

I called this "Religious Zionism," and the concept sometimes rankled the non-believers who didn't like the idea of working together with the religious folk. But I saw these two strands of Jewish life—religious and secular—coming together in Israel, tying together like tzitzit on the corner of a tallit katan.

To the secular, it seemed more like a noose.

SEEKING: ANYTHING!
CONTACT: David Ben-Gurion, Tel Aviv

I was born in Poland, which was Russia at the time, but what else is new? When I was ten years old, Theodore Herzl's *Der Judenstaat* came out, and I was so inspired, I started a club called "Children of Zion." What national-folk-redemptive ideologies did you start in *your* early tweens? That's what I thought.

When I turned twenty, I moved to an agricultural settlement in Palestine, but instead of farming (boring! dirty!), I turned to political organizing (exciting! dirty!). There were dozens of villages and farm collectives like ours throughout the land, but we could only become a country by occasionally looking up from behind our plows (no argument here!).

I went to America and raised funds, then returned to Europe to fight in World War I. After that, I began founding organizations like the Histadrut (National Labor Federation) and the Mapai political party. I don't want to say getting deep into politics was a drag, but it gave me nostalgia for the trenches of World War I.

Here's how ugly it got: I had to split with former allies like Jabotinsky and sometimes even support the British—our enemies who didn't want us there!—in order to fight the more militant and terrorist wings of Jews like the Irgun and Lehi. I was so determined to create a unified army for Israel (the IDF), I even ordered an attack on an Irgun ship that wouldn't turn over its weapons. This was one of history's most explosive examples of "two Jews, three opinions."

I also had to make alliances with those I *strongly* disagreed with. Like the religious folks, who wanted to put the whole state under strict Jewish law. I thought in the long run, we secular Israelis would outlast them (somehow not noticing their tendencies to have like eight babies per family). But I also understood their support was vital to getting this state approved in the first place. So we agreed to what was called "the status quo," which became the fixed uneasy arrangement between religious and secular Israelis that makes it one of the loudest countries on Earth even to this day.

I oversaw the United Nations' vote to partition us into Israeli and Palestinian states in 1947 (if you're just joining us now, this did not work out), the declaration of the State of Israel in 1948 when the British Mandate ended, and the War of Independence against the invading Arab nations.

As you probably have surmised, we won, and I became Prime Minister for two more terms, fifteen more years. Which in politically-volatile Israel is practically becoming president for life. Under my leadership, we turned the Negev Desert into livable farmland, airlifted in nearly a million Jews from Arab countries, and *may* have started developing nuclear weapons, though you didn't hear it from me. Oh great, now I've said too much and probably have to kill you!

Ironically, I spent my final years getting back to farming, living on a kibbutz, and writing an eleven-volume history of Israel's early years, which I will now recite to you beginning with volume one...

What's that? You'd prefer the "me killing you" option?

FIDDLERS ON THE RUN

....

IN THE LATE NINETEENTH TO early twentieth centuries, conditions became so dire for Jews in Russia, Eastern Europe, and the Pale of Settlement that millions fled Europe, seeking a better life in America. Among them were Tevye the Dairyman and his family from the little town of Anatevka. Tired of poverty, anti-Semitic violence approved of (and sometimes carried out by) Russia's tsarist government, and the relentless grind of having their most delicate emotional moments turned into giant musical numbers, Tevye, his family, and most Jewish immigrants of the time came to New York City's Lower East Side.

Since their journey had brought them so close to Broadway, Tevye and crew were inspired to create this sequel...

TEVYE
A fiddler on the roof. Sounds crazy, no?
Incredibly dangerous, extremely annoying,
Terrible pay, and zero career advancement, yes!
Not a great "survival job" for an impoverished, marginalized, agrarian people.
Even so, you may ask, why did we all leave our beloved town of Anatevka,
Our neighbors, our whole way of life behind?
Simple!
Thanks to the tsar of Russia,

Whose message to all us Jews I can tell you in one word…

CHORUS
Expulsion….
Expulsion!
Expulsion.

TEVYE
Now who would the Tsar prefer be very far-flung
As in "not in Russia,"
He don't want us here.
That's right, it's the folks who don't believe in Jesus.
He asked for us to disappear.

CHORUS
Expulsion!

TEVYE
That's it, we're moving to a place that will always welcome immigrants: America!

GOLDE
But how will we survive there? What will we live on?

TEVYE
Not to worry, my little lamb. Tevye has figured all that out!
I'll become a rich man.
Ya ba dibba dibba dibba dibba dibba dibba dum
Opportunities for everyone.
I'll be the Jewish Edison!

I'll get a job and work hard
Ya ba dibba dibba dibba dibba dibba dibba dum
Then sit back and watch the dough roll in
That's my perfect yiddle-diddle plan.

GOLDE
What about the language?
They don't speak Yiddish,
Ya ba dibba dibba WHAT?

TEVYE
We are Jews
We'll learn it, we'll adapt…

GOLDE
In one room, cold and itching,
We'll be trapped…

TEVYE
But if we stay, on us
They still will crap.

GOLDE & TEVYE
Onwards to the Pro-mised Land!!!!

TEVYE
And so, we made our journey, and the four of us ended up—exactly as Golde had predicted—sharing one room in a fifth-floor walkup tenement. I tried to make a living selling…well, whatever I could lay my hands on. And it was Golde and our two youngest, still-unmarried daugh-

ters, Bielke and Shprintze [*that's right, there's really a char-acter in the original show that no one talks about named Shprintze*], who provided us a steady income, thanks to their own masterful financial scheme.

GOLDE, BIELKE, SHPRINTZE
To sew!
To sew!
We're sewing.
Our fingers are calloused
From pricks.

GOLDE
Cause doing piecework
Is all there is.

TEVYE
Till I can launch my biz,

BIELKE & SHPRINTZE
We'll do this 24/6!

TEVYE
I've been out there
Peddling pickles,
Saving all my nickels
Till our wealth shall come.

But the pickle market's finite
Jews don't want one more bite

Of foods with sodium.

GOLDE
And so, to sew
We do it.

BIELKE & SHPRINTZE
And sometimes it's even quite fun.

BIELKE
We don't need language, or skills or loom

SHPRINTZE
Totally "Work from Room"

ALL FOUR
And so we sew on…

BIELKE
OW! My thumb.

TZEITEL & MOTEL enter.

TZEITEL
Mother, father! We just arrived from Krakow, and… wow! The New World has been good to you—and Papa's business.

TEVYE
Tzeitel, dear, so good to see you! And you're right…
(looking down at a barrel)

Was this my little pickle barrel?
Was this where I would plot and plan?

GOLDE
Now it's a store
Where we sell goods

TEVYE
And—shhhh!—*Sometimes ham!*

CHORUS
Sunrise, sunset
Expense, profit
Always on the grind.
We want our children to do better
We don't mind.

SHPRINTZE runs out, comes back in with a man.

SHPRINTZE
Tzeitel, Motel, you made it! Just in time for my announcement.

GOLDE
Announcement...?

SHPRINTZE
Everyone, meet John Gentileman...my *fiancé!*

GOLDE passes out. TEVYE mops his brow.

TEVYE: Oy, and I thought Chava's Russian guy would kill me!

GOLDE revives herself.

GOLDE
But how? How did you...?

SHPRINTZE
Melting pot, melting pot
Made me a match.
Ethnic proximity caught me a catch.

JOHN
We live next door
I walked her home from school.

SHPRINTZE
(Displaying an engagement ring) *And then one day—a jewel!*

TEVYE
A Christian?
But Shprintze, we're Jewish.

GOLDE
Come on, when
Were you last in a shul?

SHPRINTZE
Besides I'll
Stay "culturally Jewish"

Right until it is no longer cool.

GOLDE & TEVYE
Melting pot, melting pot
What did we lose?

TEVYE
Is there no place where our kids remain Jews?

GOLDE
Maybe it's time to go back to square one.
That desert where we...

CHORUS
Caàame from!

A STATE IS BORN

DIARY OF A
PRE-ISRAEL GIRL

....

1914 (AGE 12)

Dear Diary,

Happy birthday to me! My name's Anya Dawidowicz, and I live in a little town no one's ever heard of outside of Lodz, Poland. And today I turn twelve, which makes me *basically* a woman, which is why I decided to start keeping a diary. That, and because my Bubbe Dzhini gave me this for a birthday gift, and the other gift she gave me was a perfume that smells like...well, between you and me, like something rotting in Bubbe Dzhini's garden. I can't imagine wearing it (and making myself somehow even more unappealing to boys than I apparently already am), so I'm going to make a *really* big show out of using this in front of Bubbe.

Oh yeah, and also so I can record my life now because my family is moving! Pretty far away, actually. To a place in the Middle East called Palestine. It used to be called "Judea," and before that, "Eretz Yisrael," and it's where we Jewish people used to have our own country *way* long ago. (Like, even before Bubbe Dzhini's time!) Then a lot of us got kicked out by the Roman Empire, but others of us continued living there—it's just been occupied by other countries since then? It's a little confusing, but as Mama puts it, "It's still the Jewish people's old home, it's just that some other people live there now too." I hope the new neighbors have kids my age that I can hang out with—and who aren't as annoying as my stupid *stupid* little brother Janusz, who somehow manages to destroy all my stuff no matter where I hide it.

But I really don't want to leave! I'll miss my friends and my home and even my school (though I certainly won't miss Mr. Wertzberger's grammar class! Or that horrible bully *MARGY*). Still, Papa says this may be the only safe place for Jews to live, especially since some seriously scary stuff has been happening to Jews in Poland and Europe lately.

But I refuse to dwell on that on my birthday! Trying to think positive thoughts and looking ahead to the future. Even if I have no clue what that's going to look like…

1915 (AGE 13)

Dear Diary,

I can't believe I dropped the ball on you! It's just been so busy, and a lot of my stuff got misplaced during the move (that is, whatever wasn't wrecked by Janusz).

Oh yeah, so we made it to Palestine! Mama says we're actually the *second* big group of Jewish refugees to try and make a new life here. Hooray! At age thirteen, I am finally "on trend" for the first time in my life.

But it's been pretty rough getting used to our new life. We have to live in this community called a kibbutz where everyone shares the work, food, and wealth. (Ha! As if there's any of that!) It's part of what they call the *Yishuv*, the unofficial community in this patch of the Ottoman Empire that we're trying to build up into a safe homeland for the Jews. So far, this apparently mostly involves orange picking and dancing in circles.

And going to school, of course. I actually don't mind the kibbutz school. It's pretty basic, but at least there's no Mr. Wertzberger and no more grammar! Not Polish grammar anyway. Now we're learning Hebrew. But not, like, the Hebrew in our prayer books and ancient texts. Some guy named Ben-Yehuda reinvented it for the modern age to use as our official language. Which means we now have to *speak* it. Which means a *lot* of consonants where you have to do strange things with your mouth and throat. Not a day in class goes by without someone getting someone else's phlegm on them.

And I'm starting to make friends. Including a very, very cute guy from Romania named Samuel, who's caught my eye. And unlike those boys back in Poland, he doesn't seem to mind looking my way sometimes too.

Unfortunately, you know who *did* make it here? The abominable *MARGY*. She doesn't have her mean girl squad that she had back home, but she already has her eye on me too and has started making trouble.

Still, all of this definitely beats what I hear is happening to Jews in Europe right now...

1917 (AGE 15)

Dear Diary,

Ugh! Sorry, I'm terrible at keeping this up. Not helping is that Janusz and I have to share a bunk in the Children's Cabin. Even though he's ten now, his talent for destruction has only grown in sophistication. I had hidden this diary so well even I forgot about it.

Anyway, we may have left Europe, but it seems that Europe has come to us. Apparently, Britain is getting the upper hand over the Turks in the Great War and is about to take over. It's sooo confusing, because *we* used to basically be European (until the Europeans decided we weren't and made us feel unwelcome). But the British treat everyone here (us and the Palestinian Arabs, aka the neighbors) like their colonial subjects—and look down on us equally.

I wish I could report any progress with Samuel, but—wouldn't you know it—*MARGY* seems to have gotten her hooks into him. We all work together in the same part of the orange grove, but every day she has to show off something she can do better than me—climbing faster, harvesting more, even throwing out rotten oranges faster (when *she's* the rotten fruit who needs to go on the compost pile). Sadly, Sam is impressed by this, while to him I might as well just be...well, the compost pile.

The good news is that so many of us have moved here and built a life for ourselves here, the Brits have issued something my teacher says is called the "Balfour Declaration," which is like a recognition that the Jewish people can have a homeland here. They even drew up boundaries deciding where Palestinian Jews and Palestinian Arabs are going to live. Not sure if that's going to work, but it seems like the only way both our peoples can share this land.

Now if only they could draw a boundary to keep stupid *stupid* Janusz out of my makeup bottles!

1918 (AGE 16)

Happy birthday again! Although it's not exactly what I'd call a sweet sixteen. Another bombing had us all rattled last night. Even worse, they just make Janusz furious—he keeps jumping around, grabbing sticks, saying he wants to be a soldier and go fight.

I keep trying to tell him that the Arabs living in the villages around us are not our enemy, they're our neighbors. But between you and me, Diary, things are not going great with the neighbors. Some of them we've bought land from, some of them we get along with quite well, but others really do not want Jews living here. They're like, "Jews can't live here!" I'm like, "Sorry, but we *already have*. This land has had Jews and Arabs living here as long as it's had camels."

Some of them are like, "You're just colonizers!" OK, first off: I'm only sixteen, but I've already been the *colonial subject* under the rule of two empires: first the Ottomans, then the British. Neither of those empires even *want* us living here doing what we're doing—which would officially make us the worst colonizers ever. Even if we *were* colonizing, what country are we sending extracted resources back to? The invisible magical faraway nation of "Jewsylvania?"

On a lighter note, I do have a boyfriend. Not Samuel, but Alon, a nice quiet boy from my Hebrew class. It's not exactly a passion-fest, but he is such a good listener and is always there for me when this all gets to be too much. Which is basically every day.

1919 (AGE 17)

Ugh, Diary, I know I've let you down. But I had to come back and record the absolute worst thing to ever happen, even in my already-dramatic life:

My little brother may be right.

You see, things are just getting worse with our Arab... coresidents. I keep having this argument with Alon (oh yes, we are *way* past our cute "first fight!"), who calls himself a "peacenik" and believes the Arabs will eventually accept us when it's been a few decades.

But, as much as it pains me (on both the political and stupid-sibling level), I think Janusz's instincts about fighting are unfortunately right. We're not in Europe or even America. This is a tough neighborhood, we don't have anywhere else to go, and we're going to need harder edges to survive.

Not making things any easier is the fact that not only has *MARGY* fully claimed Sam as her boyfriend, she seems to be rubbing it in my face. I know we share everything on a kibbutz, but does she have to share every one of their classroom secret giggles and orange-grove kisses with *me* around the clock?

All of which makes me think, maybe I also need to fight for myself a little harder. Or at least fight for the guy I *really* want…

1920 (AGE 18)

Dear Diary,

OK, yes, once again I've abandoned you for too long. I've just been so busy! I finally got tired of the smell of oranges (or maybe just the bitterness of unrequited love). I enrolled in a vocational school, and I'm learning accounting. Numbers may drive you crazy, but they never break your heart.

Also, Janusz had his bar mitzvah kibbutz-style. I have to say, those things go pretty smoothly when literally hundreds of people are helping out and the dress code is "sandals and sun hats." Somehow Little Bro managed to make his way through the Torah reading without tearing the ancient parchment to shreds.

So where did I find the time to pick you up again? Let's just say I've suddenly got way more time than I planned to. Because all of us are currently hunkered down in our shelter thanks to the Arab riots raging out of control in several cities. We've got folks picking fights and bombing stuff and causing trouble on our side, too, but we're trying to organize them into one defense group called the Haganah. Yeah, good luck getting a bunch of Jews to stop fighting about...fighting.

Speaking of which, Janusz is practically bouncing off the shelter walls, desperate to run off and get into it with the Haganah. And Mama and Papa assigned *me* the task of keeping him out of trouble. Gee thanks, folks, I've been attempting that since before he could walk. Still, I try my level best to distract him, whether it's playing games of "battle chess," singing his favorite songs, or doing the craziest dance moves I can think of.

Finally, I get a big laugh.

Unfortunately, it's not from Janusz.

It's from *MARGY*, huddled up with Guess Who in what I thought was a hidden corner of the shelter.

Turns out there is no such thing. Even with her boy-prize solidly in hand (for years now!) she can't resist the temptation to beat me down in public again. She walks up, loudly braying like a donkey at me, saying "Well Anya, now I see why no one ever wanted you to dance the *hora*."

And then, before I can think, some inner piece of Janusz plus years of living under embattled conditions join forces, and I punch Margy, right in her evil, poisonous mouth.

She goes down like a sack of oranges. To my surprise, half the shelter applauds. They were also victims of her taunts and putdowns, but everyone was too committed to the idea of "on the kibbutz we are all one," or at least *pretending* we all believed that.

But then Samuel storms up, in a rage. Oh great, so *now* he notices me! He starts to yell, but I yell louder: "This is what you get, Samuel Frankel. For overlooking a real woman, a much better woman who's always loved you! Who...*still loves you now!*"

Now everyone in the shelter goes "AWWWW" at seemingly the same time. Guess they can still act as one when they need to. They start chanting, "Kiss! Kiss! Kiss! Kiss!" Some of them push Sam and me together. I lean back slightly, parting my lips just a tad, anticipating the taste of my final, hard-won victory.

But Sam breaks away from the crowd, saying, "Are you kidding?" He then pulls Margy to her feet and points to her belly.

She's pregnant.

The shelter residents, embarrassed at apparently betting on the wrong horse, quietly disperse. A few shout feeble mazel tovs at the parents-to-be, one of whom is wiping blood off the other's mouth.

Now it's me bouncing off the walls with rage and Janusz trying to calm me down. And then, from another hidden corner, the quiet kindly smile of Alon.

1928 (AGE 26)

Dear Diary,

Long time no write! Life will do that to you. Yes, I've moved on past the whole Samuel thing. I also finished my accounting degree. Sometimes you just have to get practical.

So now I'm working for the Va'ad Leumi, our official attempt at a democratically elected government for a not-yet-official country. They handle all kinds of government-y things like education and health care. They also make us pay taxes, which my parents never stop complaining about. Nice to see we still managed to carry some traditions over from the Old Country.

And last year, I decided to get practical in a different way. I married Alon, and guess what? He surprised me in the best way.

Remember I used to complain about him being too much of a peacenik? Well, his politics may not have changed, but apparently marriage was all it took for him to grow a spine. Now we fight all the time, and it's *glorious.*

Actually, it's not fighting *all* the time. Because now we've got a baby on the way too.

1937 (AGE 35)

Dear Diary,

Wow, it's been a while since I updated. Guess we've all been busy! There's been a big revolt by the Arabs against British rule, which we're trying to stay out of. But that's about as easy as Mama staying out of how I parent Daniel and Yulia.

Oh yeah—now we have two little ones. And not enough space for either. Ironically, they have so much in common and yet it's so impossible to get them to share. Sound familiar?

But one thing's clear—our people aren't going any-where. There's literally nowhere else *to* go. Tens of thousands of refugees are fleeing from Hitler. America is closing its doors. Meanwhile, Britain, who's still in charge, keeps making contradictory promises to both us and the local Arabs about giving us both the same land. I know the British are famous for writing farces, but they've created a real-life one with bloody consequences. And I don't mean "bloody" the way the Brits do.

The good news, if you want to call it that, is that this has allowed Janusz to "live the dream." He's taken his lifelong love of destruction and channeled it into being a munitions expert. Every week, he changes his story about which fighting group he's with. He promises they're only bombing military targets, but I'm not so sure, nor do I want to know. This is war, and it brings out the worst in all of us—but what's the alternative?

Speaking of fights, guess who got divorced. Sam and *MARGY*. You'd think that would have taken the edge off her, but quite the opposite: Now she's been coming around a lot suddenly, giving a special eye to Alon. That girl never lets up!

1947 (AGE 45)

Dear Diary,

Meetings, commissions, conferences! Nonstop bickering, impossible demands.

But enough about the Kibbutz Holiday Decorating Committee.

Seriously, it's just been nonstop since my last entry. A (second!) world war, the complete upsetting of the international order, and of course, what…happened to our brothers and sisters who decided to stay in Europe. The ones who made it out alive. They've been coming here in massive numbers. We still fight amongst ourselves, but we work as one finding them a safe place live. Sometimes I think this is like one nation-sized kibbutz, only with way bigger oranges to pick.

Speaking of, Alon has been quite successful building a business as an international distributor of Jaffa Oranges. We are very determined to become another nation that has things to offer the world, citrus and beyond. There's been a lot of religious "messianic" types in our midst, but at the end of the day, all that most of us want is the same boring, stable things of any other nation: our own roads, stamps, annoying phone company. And no one to take those things away from us as pretty much everyone in history has done.

Fortunately, there's been some progress towards that last part. There have now been multiple international discussions and declarations about what to do with the two populations who both have a historic claim to this land. The Peel Commission suggested two states, and the White Paper of 1939 promised various pieces of the land to us and the Arabs scattered throughout one state, while limiting the numbers of Jews that Britain would "allow" to immigrate.

And finally, some encouraging news: The United Nations—temporarily feeling a twinge of Jewish guilt over that whole "recent unpleasantness" with the

Nazis—voted in Resolution 181 to partition the land into an Arab and a Jewish nation. Like, official countries and all.

When that happened, there was dancing in the streets. The national kibbutz broke into a nationwide hora. Here's how ecstatic it was—I even danced holding hands with *MARGY*.

Although it was in part to keep her claws off my man.

MAY 14, 1948 (AGE 46)

Dear Diary,

Just one second for you, my lifelong companion whom I've repeatedly ditched. But you need to hear this:

I am now writing this in the officially declared State of Israel, an actual modern Jewish nation-state among the community of nations. It's an amazing moment, a miracle really, although even in this socialist country, everything comes at a price. Daniel and Yulia have both been called up to fight the four Arab nations who just declared war on us. That's right, Yulia too. We're doing things a little differently in this brand-new nation of ours.

Somehow, I have a feeling that, in the coming decades, that sentiment is going to be proven true in more ways than any of us can imagine.

THE JOKES WRITE THEMSELVES

THE HOLOCAUST (1938–1945), OR SHOAH in Hebrew, was the systematic campaign by Germany's mid-twentieth century government and its allies and subjects to separate, persecute, and ultimately exterminate millions of Jews, along with large numbers of Roma, homosexuals, and disabled individuals.

[ED: Need joke here.]

The Holocaust's origins date back to the 1920s, when Germany—still reeling from its defeat in World War I and crushing hyperinflation—suffered from unstable governance. Into this political chaos came a young man with a strongman ideology and aspirations to national office.

[ED: This is Hitler. *Do something where you undermine his tyrannical mystique by making him seem ridiculous. I mean, come on, the mustache? The stiff-arm thing? LOL city!]*

Hitler and his National Socialist (or "Nazi") party came to power in 1933 on a platform of economically restorative authoritarianism, along with the stated desire to remove the Jews from public life (and possibly expel them from Germany altogether). Although other peoples like the Roma and Sinti were also anathema to the Nazis, their campaign was primarily targeted at Jews. They declared Jews a "decadent" race that was responsible for the cultural weakness and moral laxity that caused Germany to lose the war. Not to mention being responsible for somehow creating both Marxism and capitalism.

[ED: See? There we go, finding a little cheeky irony? Baby steps.]

During this period, the Nazis implemented the Nuremberg Laws, the first in a series of statutes that banned German Jews from owning property or even having legal citizenship and forced them to wear identifying clothing.

[ED: Oh, don't be like that! If Mel Brooks, Roberto Benigni, Mel Brooks, Taika Waititi, and Mel Brooks (again) can make comedy gold out of this, why can't you?]

But Hitler and his ilk were thinking much bigger. Beginning with a surprise invasion of Poland on September 1, 1939, Nazi forces began taking over Europe, one nation at a time. In the countries under Nazi control, the same discriminatory policies were applied to local Jewish populations.

[ED: I just got your email. What the heck are you talking about—"Seems less funny at a time when some people might think this is happening again?" It's called being edgy.]

Soon all Jewish residents under Nazi rule were forcibly restricted to crowded, unhygienic, poorly supplied areas of their cities called ghettos. And in 1941, Nazi leaders introduced what they termed the "Final Solution," a series of slave, torture, and death camps across Europe, where Jews and other "undesirables" would be sent to meet their end.

[ED: Admittedly a toughie. Maybe try something about you hating to travel too? Not enough legroom? Losing your luggage? You get the idea. Let's circle back on this.]

And so, over the next four years, even while fighting the Allied Forces and attempting to expand their military reach, the Nazis and their colleagues built, maintained, and operated these camps, leading to the murder of six million Jews.

[ED: O-K, how about we shift the focus to Holocaust deniers? Now that's a hilarious, tiny, fringe, way-out-of-the-mainstream group, right? ...Right?]

As a result, approximately one-third of the world's Jewish population was annihilated, and millions of European Jews were permanently displaced from their homes and homelands, then forced to migrate to other countries. The Holocaust caused an influx of refugees into then-British-controlled Palestine and eventually the state of Israel. It also traumatized, and continues to traumatize, countless millions and their descendants and the Jewish people as a whole.

[ED: Well, so what if we're "exploiting the Holocaust for a laugh"? People have exploited the Holocaust for everything from fundraising to merch to political campaigns to every single argument online to winning Oscars to making maddening Oscar speeches. It's pretty much the only thing the world will let the Jews talk about anymore. So HAVE FUN WITH IT!]

THE MOVIE

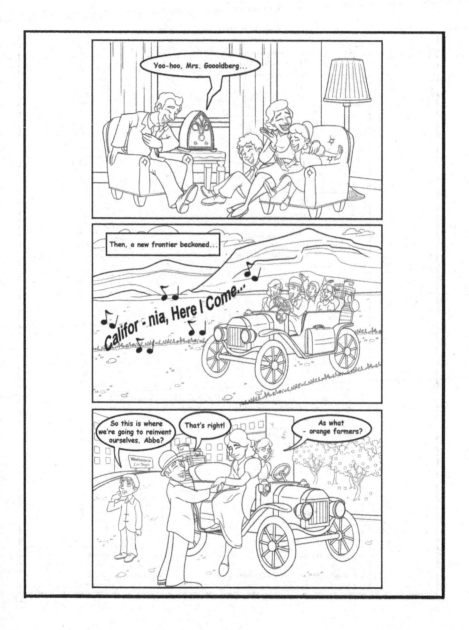

SALAAM, FAREWELL
THE ARAB EXPULSIONS

··

The establishment of the State of Israel in 1948 was considered a grave offense by the Arab nations. Many considered all of Arabia sacred Muslim land that non-Muslims were not permitted to rule. Some considered Israel a puppet colonial enterprise of the Western powers. Others just didn't do well with sharing.

In keeping with one of history's longest-running traditions, Jews were blamed. Specifically, the Jews who'd lived for centuries in their countries. So when Israel was officially recognized by the community of nations, all Jewish residents of Arab lands received this exciting offer:

SEE THE WORLD: TODAY!

Enjoy an all-expenses-paid[1] voyage to any[2] country in the world, with departures conveniently leaving every minute on the minute! No age restrictions, no blackout dates! All you need to qualify is proof of your failure to accept the one true god and his prophet!

To take advantage of this exclusive,[3] one-time opportunity, simply walk out of your home with whatever worldly possessions you can fit into a suitcase, take down your mezuzah, and be on your way!

---

1   Paid by you.
2   Excluding Algeria, Tunisia, Yemen, Egypt, Libya, Morocco, Iraq, Jordan, Lebanon, Syria, Saudi Arabia, or the United Arab Emirates. Other restrictions may apply. Pro tip: Might want to avoid Europe.
3   Exclusive to you and your fellow Hebrews!

NOW GET BACK IN LINE

1951

Lod Airport. SHULAMIT, a no-nonsense, tight-lipped female EL AL agent, is monitoring people in the security line. She waves forward the next arrival, an elderly man named YECHEZKEL.

SHULAMIT: Welcome to Israel, where are you coming from?

YECHEZKEL: Iraq.

SHULAMIT: And what is the purpose of your visit?

YECHEZKEL: It's not a visit. We're moving here. Over the past decade, our country was ruled by a pro-Nazi regime. Then there was a pogrom. Then, when Israel was founded, the government got mad at Jews and passed discriminatory laws. And recently, there was a bombing in a Jewish cafe. That's just...way too much Jewish history for one decade. Pace yourself, Iraq!

SHULAMIT: So, your purpose in moving here is to sit around all day in cafés?

YECHEZKEL: Hey, you guys were the ones who brought us here, remember? In a rescue operation called Operation Ezra and Nehemiah?

SHULAMIT: Oh no, it's fine if you sit in Israeli cafes. I just need you to promise that in those cafes, you will smoke and have way-too-loud conversations about your health problems.

YECHEZKEL: Have I mentioned this sore on my ankle, which is starting to ooze like a sack of rotten *jajeek* and—

SHULAMIT: Right this way!

1979

The renamed Ben Gurion International Airport. Shulamit gestures to a young Persian woman, FARNAZ.

SHULAMIT: Welcome to Israel, where are you coming from?

FARNAZ: Iran.

SHULAMIT: You look…sad?

FARNAZ: Yeah. Even after Israel was founded, we Persian Jews still had it pretty good in Iran. We were popular, successful, friends with our neighbors. Then the Iranian Revolution and militant Islamist leader Ayatollah Khomeini made Jews unwelcome.

(SIRENS GO OFF)

SHULAMIT: Please, come with me to the safe room.

FARNAZ: What's going on?

SHULAMIT: Terrorism alert. The Palestine Liberation Organization (PLO) has been hijacking planes, killing Israeli

Olympic athletes, and calling in bomb threats. Hey, at least there's always job security working in security!

FARNAZ: So, I'm not even safe here?

SHULAMIT: Look, this is the one place that will look out for you no matter what. And if you're Persian, your choices are either Israel or Los Angeles.

FARNAZ: Shalom, *chaverim*!

1984

The somehow weirdly ageless Shulamit welcomes a middle-aged Ethiopian man, OMARI.

SHULAMIT: Welcome to Israel, where are you coming from?

OMARI: Ethiopia.

SHULAMIT: And what is the purpose of your visit?

OMARI: Um, to escape the *famine and civil war* raging in our country? Isn't that why you guys organized this Operation Moses airlift?

SHULAMIT: Sir, I'm the one asking the questions. (checking notes) OK, civil war…so you have experience with neighbors fighting neighbors?

OMARI: What?! No, we weren't involved. It's between the government and a region called Eritr—

SHULAMIT: Too bad. Because that's something we Israelis really specialize in...

OMARI: (thinking quick) I mean...yes, of course I do! How could you even doubt such a thing. Uch, it hurts my heart that you would even *think* this—

SHULAMIT: Right this way!

1990

Shulamit calls forward a Russian teenager, SASHA.

SHULAMIT: Welcome to Israel, where are you coming from?

SASHA: Russia.

SHULAMIT: And what is the purpose of your visit?

SASHA: Nu, we tried to make it work in the Soviet Union. But then the authorities banned all practice of our religion and culture. Stalin started a blood libel against Jewish doctors. Then, when Israel was founded, we were treated as permanent second-class citizens and traitors. And ironically, when we tried to leave, the state refused, and so we started calling ourselves "refuseniks." But despite world demands to free us, we couldn't leave until the Soviet Union began to fall last year.

SHULAMIT: Whew! Did you have to make that answer so long?

SASHA: I take it you're unfamiliar with Russian novels.

SHULAMIT: I haven't been able to read one. The airline won't allow personnel to carry on anything weighing over forty-five pounds.

SASHA: So just to be candid, when we Russians get to Israel, we don't plan to be religious at all—just eat culturally Jewish foods and complain.

SHULAMIT: Then you're in the majority. Right this way!

2000

Shulamit gestures to an Argentinian couple, MARIO and ANALIA.

SHULAMIT: Welcome to Israel, where are you coming from?

MARIO & ANALIA: Argentina.

SHULAMIT: And what is the purpose of your visit?

MARIO: Our country's going through a major political and economic crisis.

ANALIA: And there's been multiple anti-Jewish bombings, including one at a JCC. That is just *way* more excitement than should ever take place at a JCC.

SHULAMIT: So you don't believe in exercise and fitness?

MARIO: On the contrary! According to the Israel Tourism Board, all anyone does in Israel is go to the beach and raves. Time to get in shape!

ANALIA: Yes, do you have a Russian novel we could powerlift with?

2030

Shulamit calls up an AMERICAN FAMILY.

SHULAMIT: Welcome to Israel, where are you coming from?

FAMILY: America.

SHULAMIT: And what brings you to Israel from America?

FAMILY: Don't ask.

WORLD REPAIR SERVICE

ARE YOU SUFFERING FROM A societal injustice? Perhaps something systemic or structural? Are your rights not coming through, even though your nation's operating instructions clearly states that "all...are created equal?" Or maybe your community or nation has been hit by a natural disaster, medical emergency, or other calamity so bad it defies all language except for insurance companies saying "no."

Time to call the Jews!

The Torah commands Jews no fewer than thirty-seven times to "remember the stranger, for you were a stranger in Egypt."[1] We also consider ourselves partners with God in the work of creation. And we're not talking passive-aggressive, microwaving-fish-in-the-lunchroom coworkers. We take our duty to fix and finish the imperfections God left in the world seriously. (Not that we're kvetching, God, but you know...)

And so, even as the world has turned on the Jews over and over again, we have always sought to right the world's wrongs, whether they affected us or not.

WORKER'S RIGHTS

In America, the flood of immigrants from Europe and China around the turn of the twentieth century[2] meant one thing

---

1   Repeated way more than the ban on eating cheeseburgers. Still unclear whether one is permitted to give a cheeseburger to a stranger.

2   The second biggest flood the Jews have been part of.

for American businesses: cheap, exploitable labor. The working conditions were dangerous and often lethal, the pay was paltry, and the hours were brutal. This was the origin of what we call the sweatshop. And it became a historic struggle for Jews—the first time they'd ever fought against a *shvitz*.

Jews like **Morris Rosenfeld,** the "sweatshop poet," gave voice to the plight of workers. **Pauline Newman** and **Clara Lemlich** and others led a historic, successful four-month general strike among twenty thousand garment workers. **Abe Cahan** founded the Yiddish newspaper *Forverts*[3] in part to translate workers' concerns into political action. And **Meyer London** got elected to Congress to fight for them. Even if anti-Semites would occasionally raise their eyebrows and ask him suspiciously, "London? What kind of name is *that*?"

Biggest Accomplishments: Labor unions, reasonable work hours, weekends off, and safe working conditions

Why? Jews know what it's like to be exploited workers (read: unpaid under the hot Egyptian sun). And we invented the Day of Rest. We've been trying to share both of those ideas for centuries. No matter how many times we get labeled "Commie Pigs."

Most Effective Chant:

> *We've got your bras and underwear*
> *You want 'em back, then treat us fair!*

CIVIL RIGHTS

Many Jews joined the Black community in dismantling American segregation and Jim Crow laws. Two rabbis, **Emil**

---

3   Which eventually became the Forward in English, or if you read it in a mirror, the Backward.

Hirsch and **Stephen Wise**, helped found the NAACP. Another, **Jacob Rothschild,** had his temple in Atlanta bombed by the KKK over his zealous advocacy for the Civil Rights Movement. Most famously, **Rabbi Abraham Joshua Heschel** was a close ally of Dr. Martin Luther King Jr and marched across the bridge at Selma with him.[4]

And it wasn't just rabbis—two of the Freedom Riders killed in Mississippi, **Michael Schwerner** and **Andrew Goodman,** were Jews. And Jewish attorney **Jack Greenberg** used the courtroom to codify the movement's gains into laws.

Biggest Accomplishments: Desegregation of schools and workplaces, anti-discrimination laws.

Why? Jews don't just identify with a history of slavery. We know what it's like to be the "other" that a nation's dominant group exploits and abuses. Black Americans' fight didn't directly affect us—Jews arguably might have even benefitted from it. Yet we immediately, instinctively saw it as our fight too.

Most Effective Chant:

> *Jews and Blacks*
> *Must unite!*
> *Now please stop making us march outside!*

WOMEN'S RIGHTS

Judaism has hardly resolved its own issues around gender. But if our world is less sexist than it was at the start of the twentieth century, Jewish women deserve a lot of credit. Women like **Ernestine Rose** and **Maud Nathan** were key fighters for suf-

---

4   The second most famous water-crossing Jews have been part of.

frage. **Betty Friedan's bestseller** *The Feminine Mystique* transformed the national discourse around feminism. In Congress, **Bella Abzug** fought for the Equal Rights Amendment and the inalienable right to wear hats the size of small moons.

Biggest Accomplishments: The right to vote, progress towards pay equity, Title IX

Why? Ever since Abraham tried to "haggle" God down from wiping out all of Sodom, Jews have always been comfortable raising their voices against the powerful. And perhaps millennia of being silenced by rabbis built up until it became "I am Jewish woman, hear me roar."

Most Effective Chant:

> *Rights for women, rights for others*
> *Do* not *make us call your mothers!*

GLOBAL AID

Israel was a nation built to welcome, heal, and rehabilitate people fleeing terrible things from all over the world. Once it got on its feet, the Jewish state started offering these services to non-Jews everywhere. Starting in the 1970s, Israel began granting safe haven to refugees in distress from all around the globe. In the 1980s, they stepped this up by flying in crews to help nations struck by natural disasters and terrorist attacks. In 1995, Israel created a permanent government agency for this purpose, while non-governmental organizations like ZAKA, Fast Israeli Rescue and Search Team (FIRST), and Save A Child's Heart have taken on search and rescue, child-heart-saving, and, um, ZAKA-ing.

Israel has also shared its pioneering desert irrigation technology with developing countries afflicted by challenging climates and its medical advances with communities who have fallen behind. Even more impressively, they've done this all without succumbing to the age-old Jewish temptation to tut their heads and say, "*Bubbele*, how could you?"

Biggest Accomplishments: Provided humanitarian aid to over 140 countries or territories, including states that still refuse to maintain diplomatic relations with Israel. Rude.

Why? From God telling Cain "The blood of your brother calls out to me" to the command to help even your enemy's fallen ox, Jews are somehow literally unable to look away. Even if a large number of them are ophthalmologists.

Most Effective Chant: No chants, because they do more acting and less talking. And for Jews, that may be their biggest self-sacrifice of all.

THE VIEW FROM THE BOOTH

DAYAN: Greetings, sports fans. This is Moshe Dayan, the long-dead commander who led modern Israel to victory throughout multiple wars.

BEN NUN: And this is Joshua ben Nun, the even longer-dead commander who took over from Moses and first led ancient Israel into...well, Israel.

DAYAN: And we have got a century's worth of military "highlights" for you today! Let's start at the kickoff: 1947! The United Nations votes to establish a Jewish nation-state known as Israel in the territory known as Palestine.

BEN NUN: Bold move, Moshe, but the surrounding Arab nations immediately got aggressive.

DAYAN: Indeed they did. We're talking a simultaneous blitz by Egypt, Syria, Lebanon, and Iraq.

BEN NUN: So...four enemies? Bru-tal! Althoooough...not quite as brutal as when *we* tried to take over the land and ended up fighting the Canaanites, Amorites, Girgashites, Hittites, Hivites, Jebusites, and Perizzites. So, *seven* enemies, almost twice as many as you...

DAYAN: Whatever, Math Genius. Point is, we beat them and got to start the country. That is, until 1967 when Egypt, Syria, and Jordan planned another invasion.

BEN NUN: Oof! That has gotta hurt!

DAYAN: It would have, but remember: the best defense is a good offense. We struck first, nailed them, and even gained some extra yardage in the West Bank, Gaza Strip, and Sinai Peninsula from them in just six days. BOOM goes the dynamite!

BEN NUN: SCORE! A Six-Day War! Almost unheard of in military history!

DAYAN: Wait, what do you mean...*almost*?

BEN NUN: Well. I'm just saying...if one doesn't count the *three* days that my troops took to crumble the walls of Jericho by doing nothing but marching around the city, blowing shofars.

DAYAN: Why do you always do this?

BEN NUN: Pro tip: Next time? Try a shofar. Oh, and those Palestinian territories you just acquired in the West Bank and Gaza, the ones full of angry people who hate you? Might want to...sort something out with them long-term. Just sayin'.

DAYAN: Thanks, Professor Hindsight. But I'm pretty sure that even *your* Israel would have been caught off guard if the enemy invaded on Yom Kippur, the holiest day of the Jewish year. Because that's what happened to us in the Yom Kippur War of 1973.

BEN NUN: We wouldn't have. Because back then all Jewish eyes were focused on the Holy of Holies, a tiny sacred chamber inside the Tabernacle (remember that portable Temple we schlepped around the desert?). We believed God dwelled there, and on Yom Kippur, the Head Priest would go in there and ask for our collective forgiveness for the year. So yeah, we were so locked in and so silent, you couldn't hear a pin drop. To say nothing of an army on camelback.

DAYAN: OK, then, we'll still take the W where we can, even if it's not in battle. Look at 1978—we signed a major peace treaty with the Egyptians!

BEN NUN: Gooooooal! That's the best thing to come out of Egypt since...us.

DAYAN: Unfortunately, it was back to war just four years later. The head of the Palestine Liberation Organization, Yasser Arafat, had been committing terrorist acts against Jews worldwide and attacking us from across the Lebanese border. So we went all...the...way...into Lebanon and established a "security buffer" there.

BEN NUN: When you say "buffer," I think you mean "protracted involvement that disillusioned an entire generation of Israeli soldiers."

DAYAN: Potato, *potahto*. But on the bright side, the 1980s brought Israel such massive inflation, we were able to create an additional security buffer made of useless shekels.

BEN NUN: Hey, did I not warn you about the whole Palestinian thing? That ain't going away.

DAYAN: Look, bub, we tried. In the '90s, we signed a treaty with Jordan and launched the Oslo Accords with the Palestinians. He shoots, he scores, he stops shooting!

BEN NUN: Right up until one of your own shot Prime Minister Yitzhak Rabin for signing that peace accord! *Foul on the play!*

DAYAN: That, and some bastards in a group named Hamas also opposed it, decided to wipe out our state entirely, and are still trying to snatch the Terrorist Olympics crown from the PLO. Ugh, I've never been more glad to be dead and buried.

BEN NUN: You know it, girl.

(*They do the world's saddest fist bump.*)

BEN NUN: But what's this? You not only kept all those settlements in the West Bank and Gaza—in the 2000s, you actually started *expanding* them?

DAYAN: Hey, you guys did a pretty thorough job of conquering the native people in your time too!

BEN NUN: True, but we didn't have cameras and white human rights activists looking for one small country to assuage all their guilt over centuries of imperialism, colonialism, and racism with in one shot. That said, the Palestinians are indigenous too, so you've got to work something out.

DAYAN: Ooh, ooh, but look, here we go: It's 2005, and we are unilaterally pulling our troops from Gaza! We are *back on the board, baby!*

BEN NUN: Only to get sucked back into Lebanon in 2006 to rescue a captured soldier. I get it. No man left behind. Respect.

(*Forget the previous one. This* is *the world's saddest fist bump.*)

DAYAN: Still, we *were* driving up the field towards full Palestinian autonomy in Gaza, when BOOM! It was *intercepted* by Hamas! They thwarted local elections, killed their political rivals, doubled down on plans to completely annihilate Israel, and started rebuilding Gaza into a tunnel-filled base of attacks. Oof! We're gonna be feeling *that* tomorrow.

DAYAN: And in 2016, and 2021, and 2023.

BEN NUN: Can we talk about 2023?

DAYAN: I'd rather not, till we see how it ends. If it ends.

BEN NUN: Well folks, that's where we are at the break. Predictions for next quarter?

DAYAN: Hard to say. Maybe someday the surrounding nations and Palestinians will accept that we're also a refugee nation of millions, we're not going anywhere, and we can all find a way to live together. Honestly, the whole region would flourish if they put guys like you and me out of business, stopped the fighting, and started trading.

BEN NUN: Whoo. Chills. Save that speech for the locker room, coach.

DAYAN: Go hit the showers, ben Nun!

BEN NUN: The what?

DAYAN: Never mind.

BAD AND/OR BADASS JEWS, AN INCOMPLETE LIST

KORACH

Background: In the Torah (Numbers 16:1–40), *after* the Ten Plagues and liberation from slavery; *after* crossing the Red Sea; *after* miraculous food, water, and military victories seeming to spring from dry sand…oh yeah, and *after* the giving of the Ten Commandments on Mount Sinai…

Badassery: …a guy named Korach piped up and publicly asked Moses, "Hey, who put you in charge, anyway?"

Legacy: Moses called on all the Israelites to "sort themselves." Either they were on Moses' side (otherwise known as "God's side)…or Korach's. Then he called on God to choose a winner by having something unprecedented in nature happen to the other group.

The Earth literally opened up and swallowed Korach and his followers. It was pretty cool, but no *Sharknado*.

Twist: Korach's sons repented so effectively against their father's actions, they are now credited as the writers of some of the Psalms in the Jewish prayerbook. Every time we sing them, you can almost hear their proud papa saying, "That's my boys!" Except that he's been dead for millennia. And again, swallowed by the Earth.

TAMAR

Background: In Genesis 38, there's a little tangent from the story of Joseph and his Brothers and the Very Cruel Game of Hide and Seek. Right after saving Joseph from being killed (so he could instead be sold into slavery), the fourth-oldest brother, Judah, went off to visit some business colleagues in the fast-growing field of sheep-shearing and marry off his sons. However, his youngest son, Er, died before he could impregnate his wife, Tamar. Judah's oldest son, Onan, refused to take over this duty for his brother (which was Jewish law back then, don't ask). God killed Onan as a punishment for breaking the law (again, don't ask), and Judah blamed Tamar for the deaths of his two sons and was afraid to have his youngest son take over Er's duty. This left Tamar in the lurch. Without producing an heir, she was effectively invisible as a woman of that time. Socially invisible, that is, not the fun, "Hey, who's making this spoon mysteriously rise through the air?" way.

Badassery: Rather than take this lack of lying down lying down, Tamar took her family lineage into her own hands! She disguised herself as a prostitute, waited beside a road that Judah frequently travelled, secretly seduced him, gave birth to his offspring, and cleverly persuaded him to support her decision.

Legacy: No one ever forgot Judah's hilarious "And that's how I met your mother" story.

Twist: Despite—or some might say because of—Tamar's extreme dedication to impregnation, her bloodline produced King David and is supposed to one day give rise to the Messiah. Not bad for one day in a costume!

YAEL

Background: In the book of Judges, while Deborah was helping General Barak defeat the Canaanites (see p. 41), the Canaanite General Sisera took a break from the battle.

Badassery: The Israelite Yael invited the tired-looking Canaanite soldier into her tent, where she offered him milk to drink, which caused him to fall asleep...which enabled her to *drive a tent spike through his head.*

Legacy: The war was over, and the land enjoyed forty more years of peace.

Twist: A large percentage of Ashkenazic Jews suffering from lactose intolerance and migraines, but it could just be a coincidence.

JUDITH

Background: In the Book of Judith (not a canonical book of the Bible), in the seventh century BCE, during the rise of Assyria's Nebuchadnezzar, a general named Holofernes planned to invade Israel.

Badassery: An Israelite woman named Judith gathered intel from Holofernes' maid about his usual nightly doings. Then one evening, while the general lay in a drunken reverie, she snuck into his tent, decapitated him, and brought his head back to her people.

Legacy: Two timeless historical lessons from both Yael and Judith:

1) Don't drink and fight Israel.

2) Don't lose consciousness in an Israelite's tent.

Twist: Nebuchadnezzar and Assyria did eventually conquer Israel. Just with one fewer head.

JESUS OF NAZARETH

Background: I mean, there's a whole book about this, quite often appended rather awkwardly to our own Bible...

Badassery: Jesus stood up to everyone: hypocrites, the corrupt, the authorities, and let's not forget the money changers. Guy did *not* like math.

Legacy: Much of Western civilization, Europe's current borders, and Elf on a Shelf.

Twist: Imagine how long this brown-skinned, long-haired socialist pacifist immigrant Jew would survive in today's America.

SABBATAI ZEVI

Background: In the mid-1600s, a boy was born to a poultry dealer in the city of Smyrna, Turkey. That boy went on to receive a traditional Jewish education, including Torah, Talmud, and Kabbalah (see p. 112), which young Sabbatai took a particular liking to. Specifically, its passages about humans invoking angels and performing miracles.

Badassery: At the age of twenty-two, he proclaimed himself the Jewish Messiah and publicly pronounced one of the forbidden names of God (no, it's not "Dwayne," though that really should be one). Though banished from Smyrna, he moved to other cities like Salonica, Cairo, Jerusalem, and Constantinople—gathering many followers and sparking a global movement.

Legacy: Some of his followers, called the Dönmeh, still exist to this day in parts of Turkey. Mostly, Zevi's name is cited as an object lesson against Jews believing in false Messiahs. See? There's no such thing as "bad publicity."

Twist: Zevi lost the rest of his followers pretty quickly when he was forced by the Sultan of Turkey to publicly convert to Islam.

BARUCH SPINOZA

Background: In 1632, Baruch Spinoza was born to a Portuguese Jewish family in Amsterdam, thereby singlehandedly demonstrating his commitment to seventeenth-century diversity. After his father's unexpected death, Baruch had to end his Jewish studies early and began studying Latin and secular philosophy with friends.

Badassery: By age twenty-two, he had become inflamed with philosophy, publicly challenging the divine authorship of the Torah and the authority of the rabbis. Spinoza was such a firebrand that he was eventually officially excommunicated from Judaism.

Legacy: Spinoza continued teaching and writing his views on philosophy and theology for two more decades, including his most famous work, *Ethics*. Although he never proclaimed himself an atheist, many contrarian Jews celebrate themselves as Spinozans rather than traditional believers. But make sure not to ask them about it unless you have a fortnight to kill.

Twist: Even till his dying day, Spinoza never stopped receiving solicitations to donate to the Jewish Federation.

KARL MARX

Background: Karl Marx was a nineteenth century German thinker whose analysis of human nature and events led him to conclude that all of history was determined by materialism and the exploitation of workers by the moneyed class.

Badassery: Marx's famous works like *Das Kapital* inspired Vladimir Lenin and his allies to overthrow the entire Russian Empire and create an aggressive ideology called communism that dominated world politics for almost a century. If you're a young person reading this now, imagine something dark and scary threatening the whole world like the Eye of Sauron. Karl Marx was its ophthalmologist.

Legacy: Decades of college freshmen wearing Che Guevara T-shirts. (Only to be later replaced by Hamas T-shirts.)

Twist: The Soviet Union and Communist states in general? *Terrible* for the Jews.

SIGMUND FREUD

Background: Vienna-born nineteenth century doctor Sigmund Freud transformed the burgeoning field of psychology. At the time, almost as little was understood about the human brain as it is now. Mostly, it was a cluster of unproven anatomical theories and superstitions, and those who suffered from its illnesses were less treated than tortured—or often locked away for life.

Badassery: Enter Freud, who said that we could solve most of our psychological issues by...*talking*. Especially talking about all our repressed sexual desires that "proper society" doesn't allow us to express. Including, but not limited to, the desire to sleep with one's mother or father.

Legacy: Made Jewish males' "mother complexes" even weirder.

Twist: Why do you feel like we need a twist? What's that about for you, *really...?*

EMMA GOLDMAN

Background: Around the turn of the twentieth century, this American immigrant from Lithuania started off working as a seamstress and ended up becoming outraged by capitalist oppression, committed to radical politics, and one of the leading proponents of the political ideology of anarchy.

Badassery: Goldman supported a famous strike in Homestead, Pennsylvania, in 1892 by scheming to assassinate the factory manager. During the economic Panic of 1893, she went to the streets, urging workers to riot. She was even friendly with the guy who actually did assassinate President William McKinley.

Legacy: Although her calls for political anarchy didn't win (unless a *lot* has happened since this went into publication), Goldman spent decades fighting many other tough causes, working against the draft, against the Red Scare, and for women's birth control.

Twist: One of her famous sayings, "If I can't dance, I don't want to be in your revolution," is most often cited by people who really shouldn't be dancing.

FRANZ KAFKA

Background: Kafka was an early twentieth century writer of fiction that vividly captures the feelings of living in a modern world of industrial and bureaucratic dehumanization. Among his most famous works are *The Metamorphosis*, about a man who awakes to find himself turned into a giant insect, and *The Trial*, about a man charged with a crime but is never told what the crime was. By day, Kafka worked for a workplace-injury insurance bureau, so he has also achieved the historic status of "Most Interesting Guy Who Will Ever Work in Insurance."

Badassery: Kafka lived in Prague, in what was then known as Czechoslovakia, which would fall under the control of the Soviet Union in just a few decades. During the Cold War, his depictions of the soulless bureaucratic state gained new relevance as a powerful cultural critique, telling the world what life was like under Iron Curtain dictatorships. And, for later generations, what it was like trying to deal with an airline company.

Legacy: The term "Kafkaesque" has become an evocative, instantly recognizable descriptor for byzantine, arbitrary institutions, practices, or rules seemingly designed to trap or frustrate. Also, it's a highly inadvisable adjective to open with on a dating profile.

Twist: Kafka was so depressive, he ordered his editor Max Brod to burn all his work after he died. But Brod thought they had value for world literature and did not comply. So even as a corpse, Kafka had his goals thwarted by a system beyond his control. Not to mention being devoured by insects.

HEDY LAMARR

Background: Born Hedwig Eva Maria Kiesler in Vienna, Hedy found acclaim early as a film actress in Europe and transferred her talents to the Golden Age of Hollywood—most famously as the star of Cecil B. DeMille's *Samson and Delilah*.

Badassery: Besides leading a bold, unashamed love life in an age of scandal (she's even rumored to have slept with Hitler!), Lamarr also had a head for science. Despite having no formal training, she helped invent a tactical advantage for US torpedoes during World War II, and later, one of the wireless technologies underlying Wi-Fi!

Legacy: Ask your grandparents to tell you about the harrowing times when we used to get our internet from a *cord plugged into a wall.*

Twist: Just imagine Lamarr living today, with teenage boys using the product of her brain to look at the…rest of her.

GLORIA STEINEM

Background: Gloria Steinem was an American-born journalist and activist who helped inaugurate second-wave feminism. (Which, as it turns out, is a lot more complicated than "being feminist while doing The Wave.") She started her career doing an undercover journalism assignment as one of Hugh Hefner's Playboy Bunnies and ended it as an international face of women's rights. Although somewhat confusingly for the latter cause, she had forgotten to take off the bunny costume.

Badassery: At age twenty-eight, Steinem and others founded *Ms. Magazine,* a then-experimental voice of the new feminism. Its premier issue sold out newsstands in eight days, and it now reaches a readership of millions worldwide. She has gone on to lend her voice to political campaigns, civil rights, LGBTQIA+ rights, and calls for peace. But so far, thankfully, not in TV ads for digestively-beneficial yogurts.

Legacy: Giving millions of insecure males yet another thing to rage about

Twist: Even when she got married in 2000, Steinem did *not* change the name to *Mrs. Magazine. Did I just blow your mind?*

SO NOW WHAT?

THE QUIZ

WHICH OF THESE ACCUSATIONS AGAINST the Jews are

a) actual historical claims by anti-Semites, or
b) made up by me?

Jews...

1. Manipulate the weather through "geo-engineering"
2. Secretly placed Jewish symbols onto Japanese currency
3. Cause earthquakes
4. Created both ISIS and COVID-19
5. Controlled the Atlantic slave trade
6. Have started every war and often financed both sides
7. Funded the "removal" of Native Americans during the 1800s
8. Make secret pacts with the Devil
9. Are secretly running the opium trade with the British Royal Family
10. Have assassinated every US president who died in office
11. Control the US Federal Reserve
12. Control secret cures for AIDS and cancer

13. Control Twitter/X's "Community Notes"

14. Started the KKK

15. Are hiding alien technology

16. Start forest fires using "space lasers"

17. Are secretly harvesting children to achieve world power

18. Killed Jesus

19. Started the Bubonic Plague

20. Do kinky sex stuff with pigs and owls

21. Are all secretly female

22. Created *SpongeBob SquarePants* to promote homosexuality

23. Developed a special strain of marijuana to turn Black men effeminate

24. Harvest and sell human organs

25. Were behind 9/11

ANSWERS: 1–25, a

POOR THINGS

As I WRAP UP THIS epic journey through time, space, and guilt, one last group of Jews is angrily demanding to be heard from. And if we've learned anything from our history, it's "Ignore a vocal group of Jews at your peril!"

So I now turn the mic over to our panel. What exactly was your (not-to-be-cooked-in-milk) beef?

Twenty-First Century American Jew: Thanks, Invisible Book Guy. Here's the thing: Right now, there's this raging (although really centuries-old) notion of the "Wealthy Jew." As if that's all of us, or even most of us. And look, there are a few rich ones, some super-rich ones. We all know who they are. Many of us spend time in buildings with their names on the side.

But I gotta tell you, *way* more of us than you could imagine are unable to buy a home, watching our wages fall behind, and still trying to pay off college loans older than a college student!

Twenty-First Century Israeli Jew: Not exactly "living the life" over here either, *chaver*...

Twentieth Century European Jew: Oh really? Did you two enjoy growing up in the country you were born in, knowing the language, and following the educational system and professional ladder as far as you could? A lot of us who, *ahem, survived* the twentieth century only did so by becoming refugees or displaced persons. Sure, we had a nice patch in the second half, but fifty years is literally 1 percent of our history!

Twentieth Century Soviet Jew: And don't forget about us, freezing in those Communist bread lines!

Nineteenth Century Pale of Settlement Jew: Boohoo. You know what *really* puts a damper on one's financial position? Having your entire home and village burned to the ground by racist assholes on horseback.

Eighteenth Century Persian Jew: At least *you* got a village to yourself. We were forced to live in the most poverty-stricken part of town—and pay a heavy tax to the government for the "privilege!"

Seventeenth Century Yemenite Jew: Ever heard of the Mawza Exile? The king forced our entire population out of our cites and into the hottest, driest part of Yemen—and that's saying something!

Sixteenth Century Spanish Jew: Oooh…getting kicked out of your cities? Try having a choice between getting kicked out of your *country* or being burned at the stake.

Thirteenth–Fifteenth Century Central Asian Jew: Wanna know what's the only thing worse than being crushed by the Mongols? Being crushed by the Mongols *twice*.

Medieval European Jew: Oh, being ravaged only two times, as opposed to "continuously"? Luxury.

Seventh Century Arabian Jew: Have you ever been the direct geographic and theological obstacle to a new religion conquering your region by the sword? Would not recommend.

Fourth Century Jew: Hey, at least you got to stay Jews. After the Roman Empire went Christian, we got the choice of "Jesus" or "severe persecution."

Second Century Jew: What's the point of staying Jews when even God's like, "Let the Romans trash the place. I'm outta here."

Kingdom of Israel Jew: You guys do realize that like 99 percent of us are subsistence farmers, right? With our entire religious calendar being "harvest-based?" In one of the driest places on Earth?

Wandering Israelite: Ooh, *harvests*. Occasional *non*-dryness. Must be nice…

Egyptian Slave: Um, guys…?

Everyone Else: Never mind. This guy wins.

A FEW LAST WORDS

FOR MUCH OF THIS BOOK, I've made a point (and often sport) of how much Jews like to argue with each other. But throughout our history, wherever we've lived, however we've practiced Judaism, and whatever language we spoke—there was one sentiment every single Jew at any time would unhesitatingly agree on...

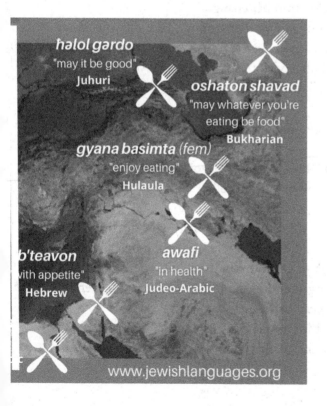

BY THE JEWISH PEOPLE'S MOTHER

Sɪᴛ, sɪᴛ, ʏᴏᴜ ʟᴏᴏᴋ ᴛɪʀᴇᴅ! What did you just do, schlep through thirty-four chapters of history? And not just any history, but *our* history. So much sadness. So much hate! So many…population number changes.

Shh, shh, ease your troubled mind. Take off your shoes. Sit back. Have a nice bowl of chicken soup/kubbeh/vareniki/abgoosht/sanbat wat. And let me tell you what your Mama's feeling…

Pride.

So much pride, my precious little people. And do you know why?

Not only because so many of you did great things. You came into existence in a world full of barbaric things like sacrifice and slavery, and turned those into…well, less barbaric versions of those things. But eventually you ditched them. And you gave the world the Ten Commandments. As well as a whole bunch of groundbreaking ethical ideas. Some, like the total debt forgiveness of the Jubilee year, are still even too idealistic for *this* era to handle!

And pssh, the people you produced, who did such great things for the world. Scholars. Scientists. Nobel Prize

Winners. *So many* doctors. Fighters for human rights and dignity. Entertainers. Athl—um, did I mention scholars?

I don't need to make a list. You can find that on your own using "The Google." Still, you know it, and history proves it: This world would be a much sadder, less enlightened, less advanced place without you. My little Jews have contributed to every field of human endeavor far above their tiny numbers. And all that while taking one day off a week!

But that's not the real reason I'm proud of you.

It's because, despite it all—and believe me, there are shelves full of history books about the "all"—you kept doing it. You kept *being Jewish*, even when the world kept telling you to stop and "just blend in." You never blended! You were like the chunk of banana in the smoothie that messes up the straw and hurts your cheeks.

And you kept teaching, learning, and trying to improve yourselves and your connection to God and each other. Even when authority figures would threaten your life, job, children, pets, and entire sense of well-being.

Well-being is overrated, I say. Well-*doing* is where it's at. And *doing* is what Jews...um, do best. Better than thinking of synonyms, anyway.

Not only did you keep on keeping on, you reinvented yourselves multiple times. A bunch of slaves became a bunch of desert hikers, who became a people with a land and a temple, who became a people without a land but with a rich portable scholarly tradition, who became innovators and builders, who became a people with a land again. History repeats itself. Just don't...go back to the slavery thing again. That was a bit of a wrong turn.

And finally, I'm proud of you because, throughout your long and painful history, you never once stopped looking for the good and trying to bring more of it into the world. A world that mistreated you so. A world that often didn't deserve it.

But mostly I'm proud, my kind, brave, unstoppable Jewish *bubbeles*, because every now and then, you remember to call your mother.

IN MEMORIAM

THE JEWISH PEOPLE HAVE ALWAYS remembered those who came before us. Even those who tried to eliminate us. And yet we remain. This wall honors their distant, *distant* memory.

Thanks for playing, haters.
Next year in Jerusalem!

ACKNOWLEDGMENTS

IT'S NOT EASY TO COVER five thousand years of history. Honestly, I don't recommend it. But if you must, you can have no greater allies than these fine people. Jewish historians Jarrod Tanny and Paul Lerner helped me get it as "close to not-wrong" as possible. Jessica Marglin, Moshe Sluhovsky. Alan Niku, and Rabbi Steve Greenberg steered me to vital sources. Rabbi Dr. Aryeh Cohen answered countless random Jewish inquiries 24/6.

I am infinitely grateful to Jacob Sager Weinstein, Todd Levin, and Stephen Levinson for their diligent reads, suggestions, and redirections. Thanks also for comedy assists from Neal Pollack, Rachel Axler, Jason Reich, and Dan Friedman; factual assists from Elad Nehorai and Michael Rothschild; and Esther Kustanowitz and Jonah Weinstein for both.

Also, a shoutout is due to Alexander Muss High School in Israel and the Pardes Institute in Jerusalem, two amazing institutions that managed to teach me a lot of this stuff...and even more shockingly, got it to stick in my brain for decades! Now if only I could remember what I noshed on for breakfast this morning...

Thanks to Adam Bellow, my editor at Wicked Son, for taking on this beyond-challenging project with me—and sticking with it, and me, even through the rough patches. Thanks also to Aleigha Koss, my managing editor, as well as Kate Harris, my production editor. Very special thanks to Judy Tashbook Safern for making the *shidduch* between us in the first place.

Appreciation always to my wife Sheryl, ever supportive as my projects get crazier and crazier, and to my kids Sasha and Jeremy for being patient whenever "Daddy disappeared into that book again."

Credit also goes to my parents, Jeanney and Steve Kutner z"l, who started showing me how to be funny at too early an age to fight back.

And finally, to my Grandpa Al z"l: Now, Grandpa. Now we eat.

ABOUT THE AUTHOR

ROB KUTNER IS AN EMMY, Peabody, Grammy, and TCA-winning writer for late-night TV (*The Daily Show, Conan*), and animation (*Teen Titans Go!, Ben10, Angry Birds: Summer Madness*). He is also the author of the humor books *Apocalypse How* (Running Press, 2008) and *The Future According to Me* (Amazon Kindle Singles, 2014), the kids' comedy-horror graphic novel *Snot Goblins and Other Tasteless Tales* (First Second, 2023), and the *New York Times* bestselling MCU in-universe Scott Lang memoir, *Look Out for the Little Guy!* (Hyperion Avenue, 2023). He has also written material for the Oscars, Emmys, and two White House Correspondents Dinners, and was named a "SuperJew" by *Time Out New York*.